ANOTHER ONE WELCOMED *home*

ANOTHER ONE WELCOMED *home*

One Woman's Journey to Finding Refuge and Redemption in the Arms of Grace

McKinze O. Berg

Another One Welcomed Home: One Woman's Journey to Finding Refuge and Redemption in the Arms of Grace

ISBN 979-8-218-44536-2

Published by Free Berg Publishing
New Auburn, WI 54757

The stories shared in this book are personal experiences and are not meant to serve as medical advice. Consult a healthcare professional for personalized guidance.

To protect the privacy of certain individuals, the names and identifying details have been changed.

Editing, cover design, and typesetting by Michelle Rayburn

Cover photograph by McKinze Berg

To my best friend, younger self, and self who knows the chapters left unwritten.

CONTENTS

AUTHOR'S NOTE

Dear readers,

I had the story all along. I just needed to put it together. Years of notes, journal entries, therapy sessions, and documents saved on my phone, tablet, and in dozens of notebooks—all coming together to provide a story. A testimony. When I was a child, there was a soap opera called *Passions*. Every single day, my mom, my grandma, and I would sit down together to watch it. Unfortunately, the series finale aired in 2008, but to this day, I can recite the ending:

> "So, after all these years, I have learned one thing for sure: Always follow your passion, because that and that alone will lead you to your happy ending."[1]
>
> —Theresa Lopez-Fitzgerald Crane, fictional character

From the time I came out of the womb, I thought helping people was my passion, even in the darkest moments of my life. Although that still may hold true, I now realize that my *passion* is being a child of God.

I pray that *Another One Welcomed Home* leads you to share your own story and helps you to find *your* passion. I'm not saying that you have to write a book, but I do invite you to share your story with someone else. To you, it may be just a story, but your story may be someone else's saving grace. My passion is leading me on the path to my happy ending. Is yours?

Love,

Kinze

Chapter 1

I'LL TAKE THE USUAL

I have told you these things, so that in me you may have peace. In this world you will have trouble. But take heart! I have overcome the world.

John 16:33

I sat in the campus testing waiting area, staring through the glass window at ten college students whose futures would change the minute they clicked the submit button. The gentleman on the left, wearing a baggy black sweatshirt, was slumped down in his chair, cool, calm, and collected.

Two seats to his right sat a middle-aged woman, most likely questioning her life decisions as she wiped the pool of tears that ran down her cheek and the snot from her nose for the fifth time in two minutes. A girl who had to be fresh out of high school, not appearing much older than the age of twelve, quit halfway through, vomiting as she sprinted out the door.

I hated test days. I could always hear every swallow, every blink, every finger tap, and every drop of sweat or tears that hit the desk. Who could ever focus? Between Randy chomping his gum louder than a cow chewing cud and Becky's fingernails hitting the back of my neck as she spit them out, how was I ever supposed to focus on answering the questions?

"Kinze? Hi, come on in!"

Pause. You may be thinking that I was next in line to sit and contemplate *my* life decisions, all while staring at a computer screen, one click after the next, wiping the tears and snot with *my* baggy sweatshirt sleeve. But you're wrong. Instead of taking a left into the testing site, I took a right into a dark room with a desk, a lamp, a couple of pictures on the walls, and three chairs. On the desk sat a black and gold plaque with JENNIFER ZUBELL, MS, along with a wire-based holder with PEACE OF MIND COUNSELING business cards. Her licenses hung in frames ever so neatly behind her office chair.

I told them I don't do this, I thought, as every inch of my body began to sweat.

"Don't do what?"

I turned fifty shades of red, and now I wanted to sprint out the door vomiting. "Sorry. Apparently, I didn't say that in my head like I thought," I sheepishly replied. I saw her lips moving, but all I could think was, *Great first impression, Berg. You're a real gem, you know that?*

She now stared at me blankly, as if I were supposed to be answering a question. "Sorry, I—"

"It's OK. I was just saying that I had talked to the two ladies you had seen before in academic advisement, and they filled me in a little bit. But I want to hear it from you."

I sat there in silence for what seemed like an eternity, staring at this stranger who didn't seem so strange. *Do I know her? Have I already met her? Why does she seem so familiar? Gosh, she's staring. SAY SOMETHING ALREADY!*

I could feel my heart beating faster and faster, the sweat rolling in constant rivers down my face. I started removing layers of clothing as if I were in the Sahara Desert, but nothing changed. *You're embarrassing yourself. Relax. Breathe. It's not that hard. Just answer the question!*

"Well, I've been struggling for a few months now with a little test anxiety," I started. "I didn't think it was that bad, but then I was in the simulation lab a couple of weeks ago, and I just lost it. I've experienced anxiety before. I've taken the meds, I've seen the therapists, and I've played the games, and nothing ever seemed to help, so I stopped. Ever since the lab incident, I can't seem to get a grip; it's never been this bad. My grades are fine, my test scores are off the charts, I'm doing well in clinicals, and I love the program. But I just don't know why I'm always so on edge. I can't sleep, I want to vomit all the time, I cry every single second I'm alone, I feel as if the walls are going to cave in at any given moment, and I don't know . . . Something is wrong with me."

She sat back in her chair and pulled out some construction paper and crayons from her desk drawer. Sliding the preschool start kit in front of me, she kindly said, "Kinze, there is nothing wrong with you. You've just hit a little bit of a wall. That doesn't mean that there is anything wrong with you. It's called being human."

"Well, I don't really do that, I guess," I replied.

"What *do* you do then?" She creased her brows.

"Well, I usually push things down, let them fester, and then explode when the bottle gets too full. Isn't that what everybody does?" I gave her a sarcastic smirk.

I took the large piece of paper and the Caribbean Green crayon, waiting for directions.

"I want you to draw me a family tree."

I barely let the poor lady finish her request before pushing the crayon and sheet of paper back to her. I chuckled a little bit, but on the inside, I was terrified. "I really appreciate what you do for people, but I don't think you understand. I just need some help with this test anxiety thing. I know how therapy works. I just need some coping skills to get through my last couple months here at the college."

There was a brief moment of silence before she pushed the crayon and paper back toward me. "Actually, I understand this quite well. That's why you're here, isn't it? You're here because you've reached that point where no matter what you do, feel, think, etc., etc., nothing is changing. You're stuck, and you obviously came here today for a reason."

I'm assuming that at this point in the conversation, my face defined "if looks could kill."

"I didn't know you were a therapist," I said in the most annoyed voice possible.

She squinted her eyes and smiled a little. "If they had told you I was a therapist, would that have changed things?"

I didn't respond, but this time, I truly thought, *Kinze, you need this. For eighteen years, you've come up with every excuse under the sun to avoid dealing with the real problems. For eighteen years, you've run from or tried to push away anyone who has tried to help you. This is enough. You need serious help.*

I picked up the crayon and, ever so slowly, began to draw on the blank piece of paper provided. As I stared at the masterpiece, a tear started to form in my eye. This tree triggered something within me, but I couldn't figure out what it was about it. I set the crayon down, gently slid the paper across the desk, and wiped a tear from my cheek. She glanced over it, and it was like watching my parents open my report card.

"Small family." She smiled.

Yep. But it's true what they say: big things come in small packages, I thought.

"Oh yeah?"

I quickly looked up, this time feeling the color drain from my face.

"You tend to think out loud quite a bit, don't you?" She chuckled.

I tried to swallow the large lump growing in my throat. "No, not usually. Sorry, I'm just a little nervous is all. I didn't like the idea of therapy before, and I don't like the idea of therapy now."

She shifted in her chair. "You don't like the idea of therapy, or you don't like the idea of what we might get into?"

I tried to speak, but nothing came out except, "I'm sorry."

"You say that a lot, don't you? 'I'm sorry.'"

I still couldn't speak. At this point, I would have done anything to get out of this room. I looked at the clock, expecting it to be past my bedtime, only to see that just one hour had passed.

"I think that's enough for this session," she said.

"This session?" my legs lost all feeling.

"Unfortunately, Rome wasn't built in a day. See you Thursday, same time?"

I stood up and nodded, again unable to speak.

As I exited the college, I had never been so relieved to get outside. I sat down under a tree and began to cry. *What are you thinking?! Are you crazy?! You don't need therapy; you're completely fine. Just get over it! Do you know how good you have it compared to the majority of people?!*

I decided to stand up and walk toward my car before campus security called for a mental health check. I got to my car, blasted the AC, cranked the radio, and headed to Starbucks for the third time that same day.

"You're back," I heard as I set my bag down at my normal spot. "You want the usual?"

I chuckled as Matt rang up the total that I had already prepared for him.

"You sure you don't want to try something else? Like maybe just a plain decaf?" He looked at me with one eyebrow raised, his beautiful brown eyes going back and forth between my trembling hands and my tear-filled eyes. I wiped the sweat from my palms, placing them in my pockets.

"How's sleep going these days? You've been here earlier than normal the past couple weeks. Everything OK? School going OK?"

Matt and I had gotten to know each other quite well over several years—in case you couldn't tell. My voice broke a little as I replied, "Of course. Everything is fine." I cleared my throat and continued. "Things are just getting a little stressful with graduation around the corner, starting a new job in a couple of months, tests, and preparing for boards. You know, the usual college stuff. I'm just a little overwhelmed and feeling a little stuck at the moment."

"Sucks, doesn't it? We've all been there. It'll be OK. See you tomorrow?" He shared a sympathetic look as he handed me my decaf coffee.

"No, not tomorrow. I think I just need some time to step away for a breather, maybe give my body some plain water for a change."

I sat in the booth and drank my coffee. I had come there to study but hadn't even opened my backpack or pulled out my laptop. I couldn't focus on anything that day. It was too noisy, and my head wasn't in the game, so I decided to do my favorite activity instead: people watch.

Have you ever watched people? I know it sounds strange, but if you haven't, I invite you to take a day to do so. You may be thinking, *Well yeah, don't we all watch people every day?* That is a true statement. We do watch people every day, but usually it's not intentional. I'm talking about sitting down in a public place and actually taking the time to observe people. About taking the time to pick up on idiosyncrasies to try to interpret or guess at another person's story, interactions, or relationships with the limited details you have.

Consider it a game of Clue, if you will, but there's no murder. Some people are very predictable. For example, Starbucks has a lot of regular customers, and usually, those customers get the same thing every time they come in. Michael always gets a "Venti black coffee with two pumps of hazelnut syrup, two cream, two sugar, and a ham and cheese croissant." Jenny always gets a "Java chip Frappuccino, no whip, and a large water." I didn't even work at Starbucks, and almost always I knew what the regulars were going to get.

As I drove home that afternoon, a thought crossed my mind. *Am I that predictable? Matt knows my coffee order by heart, and the waiters at my favorite restaurants don't even ask me what I'd like anymore because it never changes. No matter how hard I try to ask for something else, I always end up going back to the same old thing. I'll watch the same movie on repeat until I can recite it word for word, and I've read the same novel ten times in a row. Why am I like this?* I pulled into an empty parking lot, pulled out my phone, and began to type, "Why do I do the same things over and over?"

Search. Scroll, scroll, click, unclick, scroll.

STOP!

"Flocking to the Familiar under Stress." I didn't actually read the entire article. I didn't have to. The title alone was enough, but it was one sentence that stood out above the others: "Familiarity signals safety which is appealing in stressful situations."[2]

I was now crying my eyes out, snot dripping into my lap, because reality slapped me right across the face, turned my head, and slapped me again. My "I'll take the usual" meant so much more than just ordering the same food every time, watching the same movie, reading the same book, and taking the same road every day. When other people say, "I'll take the usual," they actually just really like what they get. But when *I* say, "I'll take the usual," what I'm really saying is: "I really want to try something different, but I'm a trauma kid who is just looking for something consistent in my world of inconsistencies. I'm actually really tired of this drink (or meal), but I don't want to change because change is bad. Consistency gives me control, which brings me comfort."

Over the course of the next few days, I took a little time to do some soul-searching. *Have I always been like this? Why am I like this? What happened in my life, and when, that made me turn out to be so naive?* Four days later, I drove back to Starbucks. No books, no phone, no laptop. Just myself. I had no reason to be there. I didn't have class that day. I wasn't meeting anybody. Just had the urge to get coffee. I walked through the door to see Matt standing at the register. I grinned ever so slightly. "I'll take the usual."

Chapter 2

WITHERED AND DEAD

As water reflects the face, so one's life reflects the heart.

Proverbs 27:19

"Kinze, can you hear me?"

I could hear him, but every single one of my senses was going in and out.

"Hey! Put the lights on and hit the gas. She's crashing!"

Moments later, I felt the gurney wheels crash on the ground as they tore me out of the back of the ambulance.

"Kinze, keep your eyes open, darling! Let me see those eyes!"

We passed through the doors. Too many voices. The lights in the room were so bright. I stared at the ceiling tiles, my head feeling foggy. I couldn't lift it off the pillow.

Is my blood going to be up there next? Did the last guy make it? Can I at least say goodbye to my family first? All these questions circled my brain, but what I heard next was enough to revive anyone in the crashing moments.

"How far out is her family?! Somebody call them and get them on speaker! Call the OR and tell them we're on our way! We're cutting it close, guys. Let's move!"

I couldn't tell who was giving orders, but I knew this was serious by their tone.

I've been here before—multiple times—but this time is different. Is this it? Is it finally happening? I thought I was ready, but now I don't think I am!

"You just hang on, baby girl, we're on our way! It's not time! Kinze, you hold on! Do you hear me!?" I heard her voice in the distance. A voice of sheer panic. A voice of a mother about to lose her daughter.

I was too weak to speak. *I hear you, Mom. Loud and clear.*

I didn't remember entering the cold OR suite. I didn't remember getting put to sleep. I didn't remember a whole lot of anything that day except the doctor's last words: "We got her, just get here safely. She said she loves you."

I lay there awake on a cold, hard hospital mattress, unsure of the day or time. *Am I alive? Why are my arms taped? Why are there so many alarms sounding? Why do I feel like I got hit by a train?* I looked around for a clock, but all I could see were the lights from the hallway peering through the glass sliding door of the room.

Everything is so foggy.

I couldn't see straight, but in the distance, I made out the sign above the entrance: MARY BRIGH INTENSIVE CARE UNIT 7.

I took a deep breath. *OK, guys, I hung on. Where is everybody? Hello?! Is anybody out there?* I tried to sit up. Every staple, stitch, and bandage pulled against my skin, causing me to sink back into the bed as if I were restrained. I pushed the call light button and waited for someone to come. Nobody came.

Maybe I did die. What if they lost my body, and I'm never found? Or worse, what if they thought I was dead, but I'm alive, and they told my family I was dead? Or what if this is where they send patients whose prognosis is terrible and their families don't want them anymore? What if . . . ? What if . . . ?

The alarms grew louder. More persistent. *Please make them stop.*

A nurse came running in to silence them.

Maybe it's the anesthesia, but she's gorgeous. I'm not attracted to the same sex, but I can appreciate and recognize a beautiful woman when I see one. She appeared to be in her forties, stood about five feet tall on a good day, had long dark brown hair that glistened in the light. Her big, beautiful hazel eyes stood out behind her thick, sophisticated black glasses. She had to stand on her tiptoes to reach the monitor, but her short stature didn't stop her.

"Welcome back to earth. How nice of you to join us! How are you feeling? I gotta give it to ya, kiddo. You know how to fight, that's for sure," she said.

I could feel the dazed and confused look on my face, but as I began to speak, the glass door slid open, and I recognized some familiar faces. Most people begin a conversation with "Hi! How are you?" but mine was a bit different this time.

"How close?" I asked as my mom kissed my forehead.

The surgeon stood there with his hands in his white coat pockets. "Too close for comfort if you're asking what I think you're asking."

Mom's hands trembled, and her lips quivered. Tears built up in her eyes as her color went white as a sheet. "We thought—" She had to stop. The thought of speaking such words pained her to no end. That was written all over her face.

I stopped her mid-sentence. "But you didn't. I held on." *For some reason, I always hang on.*

A feeling of rage now built inside of me. I remembered the terrifying feeling of not wanting to die. But it's almost as if I was disappointed that I didn't. I thought that if I had died on the table, I wouldn't have to be the one at fault, or to blame, for my own death. It's a selfish feeling, but I didn't want to do this anymore. Weeks had gone by.

I thought this feeling would go away, but it won't.

Six weeks later, I was headed home. It was a very awkward, quiet two-and-half-hour ride. *Do we talk about what happened? Do we ever talk about what happens when we go through this? Or do we just continue going through life as if everything's fine?*

From this moment, and even all the times before, I felt in my heart that it was my duty to make sure that everyone knew and, more importantly, thought I was OK. I took it as my duty to make sure everyone else wasn't too traumatized by the series of events that had just occurred and, for some reason, kept occurring. Let's face it. I really cut it close this time. Was I struggling? Absolutely. By the thirtieth time, it should be easier. Everyone said I was a pro, but it kept getting harder.

Make it stop. Just please make it stop.

It all started in 1998. A precious little baby was born with (at the time) a very rare birth defect called gastroschisis, a birth defect in which the abdominal wall does not form during the cooking process. The digestive and surrounding organs are on the outside of the body rather than being tucked away nicely in their original spots inside of the body.[3]

Yes, I was born an alien. No, I do not identify as one in 2024.

They ripped me away from my parents, filleted me like a fish, shoved the organs back in the best that they could, sewed me together like a ripped teddy bear, slapped me on a ventilator to help me breathe for a few weeks while I fought to survive, and said, "She's good for now. Good luck!"

Over the years, this condition left me with a great deal of complications, surgeries, and an overwhelming number of medications to take daily. At the young age of twenty-five, I had over forty operations, and although it is completely unknown at this time when or if I'll need another, I'm doing what I can with what I have to work with. I'm thriving now, but it wasn't always like this.

For those of you who have suffered with lifelong medical problems, you know there is something about being hospitalized so many times that, after a while, you throw in the towel. I didn't know this, but it's a real problem when you have a "to-go bag" that stays in your vehicle year-round. It's a problem when you're on a first-name basis with the ladies in the gift shop in another state, and apparently, it's a problem when you get a Christmas card every year from Jerry in Environmental Services. I wasn't aware that this isn't a "normal, everyday life" thing. Who knew?

I became used to living out of a bag. Living within the same four walls for weeks at a time. I was always ready for whatever was thrown my way. But this time was different. I was mentally unwell on top of being physically unwell, and I was hurting in ways I couldn't comprehend. I stopped trying to wrap my head around it all the moment I walked out of that hospital room.

After that round of events, I basically gave up on the idea of living. Not that I ever really felt that I was living in the first place. The previous years were a living nightmare: one surgery after the next, one infection after the next, one medication and test, and, and, and.

At this point, I really would have rather been dead than to continue living a life of lies. Internally, I was bitter, hateful, and resentful. But externally, I was a broken record player:

"Yeah! Things are going really well!"

"I'm feeling much better; we just have some more tests to run."

"Yeah, it's really hard to know when and if it's going to happen again."

"No, they haven't found a way to fix it."

"Yes, I'm so grateful to be alive! Really, everything is going smoothly!"

"I know. God is so good! You're absolutely right!"

The last time I said, "I'm grateful to be alive," or "Yes, God is SO good," I could have puked. It seemed so incredibly forced at this point. *Are they buying what I'm selling? They seem to be, so just keep rolling with it, I guess.*

A few weeks passed, and I returned to work. Believe it or not, I am one of the few who can say "I love my job" and actually mean it! At least, that's what I thought prior to all of this. I'm a respiratory therapist by trade. When I tell people what I do, their automatic response is, "That is awesome that you have the ability and gift to help people breathe! What an incredible job to have!" It's true! Being a respiratory therapist is probably the hardest but most gratifying thing I've ever done!

I've treated people on the worst days of their lives, and I've treated them on some of their best. I've held children who've lost a parent, and I've held a parent who has lost a child. I've heard the agonizing cries and screams when doctors give someone the worst news of their lives, and I've heard the first breath taken after the surgeon gives the "They're going to make a full recovery" speech. I've placed people of all ages on machines to help them breathe, and in the very room next door, I have removed someone else from that exact same machine. Being a respiratory therapist is not for the faint of heart. Working in medicine, in general, is not for the faint of heart.

After going back, I found myself asking the same questions over and over. *Is this what I want to do? Am I happy with where I'm at? Is it even worth it anymore? Is anything worth it?*

I can't count the number of times I had a resignation letter drafted to hand in on a Monday morning. Unfortunately for me, I never had a backup plan that didn't involve driving my car off the road or taking a handful of pills to take away the pain. So, instead, I got up in the morning, drank my coffee, and said, "Today will be better."

Except it never was.

I'd go to work, and I went about life, but the days weren't better. If anything, they seemed to all blend together. My attitude was terrible, and I always felt out of control. But even in the midst of my feeling out of control, people asked the same questions. "How do you do it? How are you so calm in every situation? How do you go through life so carefree without worries?"

I had already answered my own question: Is my act believable? *They're definitely buying it. Keep up the good work!*

As the months continued on, I started to notice that I felt completely drained all the time. I wasn't eating. Sleep was non-existent. My mood was terrible and unpredictable, and I felt as though I was standing still amid a moving world. I was becoming the type of person I swore up and down I would never become, and now I hardly recognized myself. When it came to work, I pulled into the parking lot of the hospital and absolutely dreaded having to enter the building. I was becoming frustrated and, to be honest, quite jealous. I took care of patients every day who, just like me, didn't ask to be put in a certain position but were anyway.

The babies and children I saw at work didn't wake up each day and say, "Hey God, it's me. I just wanted to let you know that I could really stand to struggle with my breathing today. Thanks in advance." Or what about the college football player that had dreams of going to the NFL but is now confined to a wheelchair for the rest of his life because of a drunk driver? He *may* have asked for it, but I'm going to say that I'm 99.9 percent sure he didn't.

We also have return patients who we saw last week when we told them, "You need to do ABC."

They looked at us then and said, "Well, what do you know? It's my life. I can do whatever I want."

They left, did XYZ, and now their medical team is left beating our heads against a wall because they can't get a grip on how precious life is. Maybe it was my own internal crisis speaking—a sense of jealousy completely taking over. I would trade anything to be in a situation that could be fixed with putting down a cigarette, taking medications that would actually take care of the problem, or not going on a drinking binge every other day. How could someone be so careless with a situation they could control?

A few more weeks passed, and I thought I was doing OK. I was overwhelmed but doing the best I could. My trauma continued to pile up, and it was getting to a point where there was no longer just a crack in the foundation. I began to spiral, and I woke up one morning realizing that the entire building had collapsed.

This frustration, and every other emotion I was experiencing, was not just work-related. The problem was most likely never work-related to begin with. I felt withered and completely dead inside. Instead of opening my eyes in the morning and starting each day with a grateful heart, I started my day hating that I was going to be on this earth another minute.

Instead of "Now I lay me down to sleep," I prayed, "Please, Lord, not another day." There were all these people in the world doing terrible things and getting all these breaks in life. Meanwhile, I was over here doing everything I was supposed to, crying myself to sleep, screaming into my pillow so loud I hoped my family couldn't hear a single word. *GOD, CAN'T YOU HEAR ME?! I have remained faithful to you. I've done everything you have asked. I've served deserving and undeserving people on my best and worst days for over two decades. I've read your Word. I've gone to church. I've done everything! WHAT MORE DO YOU WANT?*

I woke up one morning as a completely different person. *How can one have a pulse if they are no longer alive? How can a heart still beat if it's as black and cold as a winter's night?* I had gone from a young, Christ-driven woman to a lone wolf who couldn't believe how foolish she had been for believing that there was ever a higher power for over twenty years.

I stayed in that coldness, that loneliness, that rut, for I couldn't even begin to guess how long. I was miserable. My health continued to decline. I was promised five to ten years at best. There was absolutely no surgery that could save my life. If they'd tried, there was over a 50 percent chance that I'd never make it off the table. I was willing to play the game, but my family was not. After that, my mentation completely disintegrated. I was going insane, and I truly felt that at this point, I'd be better off in a psychiatric institution or, better yet, dead.

Hiding it from my friends and family was easy until it started to weigh so heavily that I couldn't hide it anymore. I stopped sleeping altogether. Stopped taking care of myself. Stopped communicating with friends and family. I no longer had any idea as to who I was. My reflection in the mirror was someone who just happened to physically look like me. I lost sight and touch with everything and everyone. God included.

And there I was, adrift in the ocean of emotions, health challenges, and thoughts without the resources to kick or paddle to safety.

Think back to learning how to swim in a pool. If your parents had similar parenting styles to mine, it probably won't surprise you when I say, "I don't know. They just kind of threw me into the pool one day and said, 'Swim!'" Well, that's not exactly how it happened. Fortunately, my parents put me through swimming lessons, and I was "always a natural," as they'd say.

I was an excellent swimmer. But every good swimmer, or even one who can't swim at all, knows that if you're in the middle of an ocean without any flotation device, it doesn't matter how great of a swimmer you are. If the waves are strong and powerful enough, you will get swept under.

Unfortunately, it took me quite some time to realize that in all those years, God was my flotation device. I thought I could go without, but I couldn't.

It's just like back when I was in the fifth or sixth grade, thinking I was cool enough to wander around Walmart by myself. We went every week or two. It was the same routine, so it couldn't be that hard. Mom would let me go off on my own, and after looking around, I would think, "Geez, there are some sketchy people in this place."

Every week looked like this, and every week, I would wander up to the customer service desk, asking Sally to page my Mom overhead. "Attention Walmart customers: Shannon Berg, please report to the customer service desk to claim your daughter. She's almost a teenager and apparently has the world figured out, but she's scared of the people of Walmart. Good luck with this one!"

Parents of teenagers with a new driver's license may know this scenario: you receive a phone call from your child, and you pick up. "Hi sweetie! Everything OK?"

You hear the snot, tears, and hyperventilation from the other end. "Can you come get me?"

Well, that was me. The snot, the tears, all of it. Yes, that was me at some point in my life with my earthly parents, but as you've probably gathered, I'm not talking about them. I needed my *Father*! My *heavenly* Father! Let's face it; I knew exactly what I needed the whole time, but I didn't want everyone to be right. I didn't want my *Father* to be right. Every child knows that one of the worst things in the world is your parents being right and saying, "I told you so." I didn't want God to do the same thing, so I found every way to dodge him.

At this point, you may be scratching your head, thinking, "Why in the world wouldn't you just ask for help?"

I thought about it, but it wasn't that easy. The truth is that I didn't want or accept help prior because there was nothing that could be said or done that I hadn't already tried to get me out of this situation I was in. I even went as far as cutting my relationships with my Christian friends and family because if I heard "You just need to pray and trust God more" one more time, I was going to take their Bible and beat them over the head with it.

One morning, I sat in the work parking lot, ready to get the day over with. I already had it in my mind and heart that it wasn't going to be a good day. *Even if it is a good day, I'm going to make sure it isn't. I'm not deserving of anything good at this point. If someone doesn't say "good morning" back to you? Day ruined. Bathroom out of toilet paper? Day ruined. Clock crooked on the wall? Day ruined. If there is any bit of peace in this day, get rid of it. It's not going to last anyway. It never does.*

Later in the afternoon, a tough case had just been airlifted to a nearby hospital. The case pulled at my heartstrings a little too hard, and I felt the emotions rise. *Take a walk, Kinze. It's OK. Take a walk.* I continued to hold back the tears. Those of you who know me personally know that although I'm an emotional person, I'm very rarely an emotional person in the work environment. It creates a disturbance in my professional and personal life and becomes unhealthy for me.

Like many healthcare workers, I thrive in stressful and fast-paced environments, but this particular day was different. It felt as if it were my first day on the job, and I wasn't the only person to notice.

As I cleaned up the trauma bay, I heard her peppy steps come through the door. Angie, my "mom in Christ," is a beautiful woman God placed in my life—a Christ-driven woman I've had the privilege to not only work with but become best friends with. A woman who has been with me through many seasons of my life, has sat with me in the mud, and pulled me out of the darkest place of my life. Saying that she has been a huge part of this journey, this story that you are reading, would be an understatement.

I waited to hear papers shuffling or drawers closing or typing on the keyboard, but all I heard was silence.

"How about tonight, after work, I take you up to the cabin and show you around? You can follow me there. It won't take long at all," she said at last.

I stood with my back turned to her, thinking about my next move. *Seriously, Ang. The last thing I want to do right now is go and see your fancy cabin.*

"Sure," I said. *What do I have to lose at this point?*

I waited at the corner store until I saw her red vehicle pull to the stop sign. With my music cranked, I put the car in drive and began following her down the road. I started to regret my decision. *What are you doing? This is stupid. Just go home.* I cranked the music a little louder, trying to drown the thoughts.

About half an hour later, we pulled into a driveway that could have led to Narnia. I put the car in park and sat for a few minutes, contemplating whether or not I should get out or just turn around. She jumped out of her car and started walking toward the dock. I turned off the engine and exited the vehicle, standing in awe of the view right in front of me. She kept talking, but the sound coming from her mouth faded. I saw her lips moving a mile a minute but didn't hear a single word.

This is beautiful.

I walked toward the dock, and with each step it felt as if I were going further underwater. *My chest is getting tight. I can't breathe.* I tried to speak, but nothing came out. Angie turned around, and without saying a single word, grabbed me and pulled me in tight. I collapsed into a pool of tears. She brushed the hair behind my ear, wiped a tear from her cheek, and placed her hand on mine.

"Hear me out. I want you to stay here. Three days. That is all I'm asking. Just bring your Bible. You don't even have to open it. Bring your journals, your guitar, and just give me three days. Something is going on, I don't know what it is, but I know exactly who you are, and this is not it. Please."

As I drove home, I couldn't stop thinking about our conversation. *You have to do something, or you're not going to make it this time.*

A few weeks passed, and I found myself traveling down a familiar dirt road. Dust billowed behind me in the rearview mirror, and I felt the rocks kicking up beneath my wheels. At last, I put the car in park. As I unloaded the bags, all this anxiety and hesitation came over me. The root of my fear was being scared to be alone with my own thoughts in the most uncertain of times. I dropped the bags at the door and stood there on the front porch, unable to move. I couldn't unlock the door.

It was quite simple. Step one: approach the door. Check! Lift arm, insert key, turn knob, and that was it! It wasn't rocket science.

I stood here a little while longer and thought for a moment. *This is ridiculous! This is the dumbest idea you've ever had. You don't need to be here. You're fine. You're overreacting. You're just in this rut, and it's just going to take some time. Turn around, load the bags back into the car, and go home! You don't belong here. You don't belong anywhere!*

I tried to turn around, but I couldn't do that either. My feet had imaginary cinder blocks strapped to them, and neither leg would function. I began to panic, and I finally lost it. Then, like any normal person would do, I looked up and started screaming at the sky.

"YOU WIN! Are you happy? DO YOU HEAR ME NOW? I get it, OK? Whatever you want. Whatever I'm supposed to learn or do here, it's yours! Just make this stop! I can't do it anymore!"

I sobbed, feeling as if I'd just run a marathon. I pulled myself together and looked around to make sure nobody had witnessed this freak show spiral out of control. As I caught my breath, trying my best to relax, I noticed I felt as if nothing had happened—as if I didn't just have a complete mental breakdown in the middle of nowhere. That couldn't have been any further from the truth because, in this moment, everything happened.

In this moment, I felt my soul leave my body, and this overwhelming amount of peace overtook me. *I've never experienced this before. I hate it. I feel so uncomfortable.*

Maybe it's growing on me? The feeling of peace. I stood there a little while longer to soak it all in.

Wait. What's happening? My shoulders dropped, and what had been a clenched fist at my side was now an extended hand to an old friend. *All right, buddy ol' pal, here we go.*

Three days. Three days of peace, music, and eventually Scripture, once I put the stubbornness aside. In seventy-two hours, I reminisced on twenty-five years of good, bad, and everything in between. Three days without contact with the outside world. With every memory I thought of, I accepted the emotion and feeling that followed and prayed on it. I've never felt so free in my entire life, and it's an experience I will forever be grateful for.

Under the title of this chapter is one of my favorite verses from the book of Proverbs. "As water reflects the face, so one's life reflects the heart." Just as the calm water shows a reflection, and a mirror displays your image, so does your heart reveal your identity. I thought I knew Jesus. I thought I had a relationship with him growing up. But the truth is that all I had was an unhealthy relationship with myself. I had an unhealthy relationship with everyone and everything around me. I realized that I knew *of* Jesus, but I didn't actually *know* him. I had no idea.

Before discovering Christ, my identity—the identity I believed—was the "walking dead."

My heart was withered and dead.

Everything about me was withered and dead.

Was.

Chapter 3

IT ALL STARTED WITH A DREAM

Not one of all the LORD's promises to Israel failed; every one was fulfilled.

Joshua 21:45

"You seem like you're lost."

I look at him, confused. "Excuse me?"

He stared a little longer. "It's almost like you don't know or understand who you are."

I had never told anyone how I truly felt, so I was taken aback when a complete stranger took it upon himself to make such a statement in the middle of the liquor aisle.

"What do you mean?" I ask him.

"You haven't found your true self yet, have you? You're searching for something that you can't put your finger on. You need to be set free to find your true identity."

I paused in disbelief, feeling as if he had just read my mind. I had been looking for something that I couldn't quite put my finger on, but the reality was that I was afraid of being set free.

"What happens when I'm set free?" I asked, slowly putting the vodka bottle back on the shelf.

He patted my shoulder and walked away. "You'll know."

The Duluth Rose Garden in Duluth, Minnesota, is potentially one of the most beautiful places I've ever visited. If you've never had the opportunity to see it in person, I highly recommend it. It's a garden filled with a variety of beautiful flowers, and even on the hottest of days, their beauty doesn't change. I may not have the greenest thumb, but I do have a "green eye," meaning I can recognize and appreciate when agriculture is well taken care of.

Attached to the garden is a lake walk that leads to just a portion of Lake Superior. Although you may not find this fact overly fascinating, I think that it's amazing that the world's largest freshwater lake is located just one hour from my driveway.

I'm going to take a moment to talk about a rock. Yes, a rock. You might be thinking, "I'm not here to learn about rocks, or lakes, or even gardens. What were you smoking when you wrote this? This book blows!"

Hang in there, folks. I'll get to the point. Just give me a chance. This place has a billion rocks; they're all over. But the first time ever going down to the lake, I noticed *the* rock. It's solid. Before you ask, "Aren't all rocks?" let me say, yes, of course they are. But this one is different. This rock is not just solid, but it has a firm foundation and sticks out. It sits in freezing cold water year-round yet stands tall and is not affected by the strong, powerful waves that crash against it. It remains consistent in an inconsistent environment, just like the flowers in the garden remain beautiful despite the storms they encounter.

"So, what's the point here, Berg?" you ask.

The point is that if rocks and flowers can withstand the strongest and most powerful storms and not be affected, why can't we?

As a child of God, I've learned that it is important to remain consistent in the inconsistencies of this world we live in. Sometimes it's difficult, but as long as I am well taken care of, and my mind, heart, body, spirit, and soul are open to the endless possibilities our Creator has in store for me, I can always remain consistent in the inconsistencies. The good news? You can too.

The first full week of July 2023 felt overwhelming. I had just been released from the hospital a couple of weeks prior. I also felt that my relationship with Jesus was at a standstill. My heart felt heavy, and I didn't feel as though the Holy Spirit was near. The following Sunday after being released, I went to church and felt nothing. It was a terrible feeling, but I could not feel the presence of Jesus Christ in the room that day.

My Bible readings didn't make any sense. I didn't get into the worship music or take anything away from the sermon. I didn't want to associate with anyone. I was distracted and took my eye off the prize. See how easy it is?

My reflection in the mirror that Sunday after returning home from church looked and felt like death warmed over. I had willingly worked almost every day that week because of greed. Other than being home long enough for maybe a meal and a nap on one or two days off, I expected myself to be able to drive full speed ahead on an empty tank. I'd lie down for a nap, and two seconds later, something I forgot to do days prior popped into my mind. I recognized this feeling and didn't like it. Nor was I going to allow it to enter back into my life.

Early that evening, I gave in and took the white cap off the orange bottle. *Nighty night.* I lay in bed staring at the ceiling, knowing that in about an hour, I'd be down for the count, and seventeen hours later, I found myself gasping for air, drenched in a pool of sweat.

Breathe. It was just a dream. You're OK. You're safe. It was just a dream.

I walked to the kitchen to grab an ice pack to cool myself down. Then I changed my sweaty pajamas and stood staring at the empty bed that now held the damp outline of my body as if it were part of a crime scene.

It was just a dream. It's not real. You're just crazy.

I couldn't wrap my head around what just happened. It wasn't just a dream because there has only been one time in my life that I remembered a dream, and it unfortunately came true. I grabbed my journal and began to chicken-scratch across the pages before the memory of it was gone. When I finished, I began to cry. I haven't remembered a dream that vividly in fifteen years. In fact, I haven't remembered a lot of things in fifteen years, including the majority of my childhood. I sat on the couch in the empty living room with my cup of coffee and began watching the play-by-play flash before my eyes.

I was back at Lake Superior, but how did I get there? How did I get to the shore? There was no lake walk, and there didn't appear to be a way back up to the garden. I looked up over my shoulder, and the flowers were so alive. But I knew I wasn't here for the flowers. I was there for the rock, and in order to get to it, I'd have to do the unthinkable by stepping into the water.

The water was colder than a Finnish winter. The pebbles on the bottom pierced the soles of my feet like razors, and my teeth began to chatter. I continued into the water and climbed up onto the rock to sit. The view was absolutely breathtaking, but I sat thinking, "You idiot. You could have gotten this same view in any other place, yet you wanted to almost drown yourself and die from hypothermia just to get to a stupid rock?"

Yes. No other area brings me the peace and comfort that this rock does.

I checked the temperature on my phone. It was sixty-eight degrees. The sun hit my face, and I closed my eyes, listening to the waves crash against the rock beneath me. The powerful waves didn't scare me because I knew I was seated on a firm foundation, and nothing could ever destroy it. Suddenly, the hairs on the back of my neck stood up, and I had this feeling that I was being watched. My eyes popped open, but nobody was there, so I gently closed them again. Moments later, the same feeling occurred. I opened my eyes, and there was a man standing in the distance, but I couldn't see his face.

He began to speak, but it was only whispers.

"Please come closer. I can't hear you. I can't see your face."

He didn't come closer, but his voice became louder. "What are you waiting for?" he asked.

I stared at him, confused.

"What are you waiting for?" he shouted a little louder.

I could feel the tears begin to well up in my eyes, but I wiped them before they had the chance to fall. "For you to guide me. I'm stuck, and I don't know what to do. I don't want to stay, but I can't leave. I can't hurt them," I replied.

"Do you know who I am?" I felt a gentle hand press on my lap. A brief pause. "I know who I am, and I know who you are because you are mine, and mine alone. You are a part of me, and because you are a part of me, I am a part of you."

"But I left!" I screamed.

Leaning in a little closer, he whispered in my ear. "But you came home. I called you by name, and you made the decision that it was time to come home. Do you trust me?"

I was faced with the dreaded question. "Of course!" I replied.

"Then what are you waiting for?" He stood ever so slowly, looking into the water. As he walked away, the water began to ripple. "What you are about to do is going to hurt, but do not be afraid because I am with you. You're going to have to trust me, but I want you to do something so unimaginable that you become unrecognizable. You have to break the chain, and when that chain breaks there will be open wounds, but they will heal with time. The pain will be severe, but keep your eyes focused on me, and just trust me." His back was turned, and he continued to walk away.

"Why are you doing this?" I shouted.

But it was too late.

He was gone, but the ripples remained. I looked down to the water beneath me, and the voice was not a man's but a woman's. One that was incredibly familiar. "Three days, that's all I'm asking. Three days, that's all I'm asking. Three days, that's all I'm asking."

It sounded like a broken record, but suddenly it stopped. The memory in the water was gone. I looked up, and everything was gone.

No trees.

No people.

No lake.

It was just me on the rock. *Hey, what happened to the sunshine? Why is it so foggy?* I stared into the distance, but I felt as if I were sinking. I looked down, and what I believed was a firm foundation was now crumbling beneath me. And then, I was submerged in a body of cold water.

I screamed, but nothing came out of my mouth.

Now, I sank down further and further, feeling the life drain from my body. I looked down and saw the chains strapped around my ankles, the weights too heavy. Reaching down through the frigid water, I tried to undo them but couldn't.

The strength was leaving me. Cold water entered my lungs, and second by second, the ability to hold my breath ebbed away. A heaviness overtook my entire body, and I began to feel my body shutting down. My eyes began to close, but I could see something in the distance. Then sounds. But I couldn't make out the words.

"I hear you. Come closer! Come closer. PLEASE! Can you hear me? Can you see me? I'm over here! PLEASE HELP ME!" I tried to scream.

The shape grew bigger. *He* was getting closer. I was now face-to-face with the faceless. "NOW! BREAK THE CHAIN!" he screamed.

I reached down to tear the chains away from my ankles, watching part of my flesh sink to the bottom of the water along with the shackles. I kicked my feet as hard as I could to reach the top. *It's too far. I'm not going to make it.* I felt a strange pressure against the bottom of my feet, so I used it to push off as hard as I could. I screamed my way to the top, hearing a voice in the distance. "You just hang on, baby girl."

Mom?

GASP

A few weeks later, Angie and I were back at the cabin.

"Angie, I have to share something with you. It's actually really freaking me out. I can't stop thinking about it, but if I try to talk to anyone else about it, they're going to think I'm crazy. I had a dream." I said it as if nobody in the entire universe has ever had a dream.

"Oh yeah? Have you never had one before?" she asked with a confused look in her eyes.

"No. I mean, yes, I know people dream. But Angie, I've only remembered a dream that vividly once in fifteen years!" I said as she got comfortable on the island stool.

"Fifteen years? That's a long time! Well, let's hear it," she said in excitement.

I read her my journal entry, and we both stayed silent for quite a while. Reading that to her was as if it had never left my memory; everything was just as real as it was when I wrote it.

"Kinze. I don't even know what to say." She paused. "I'm absolutely speechless!"

The next morning, we both got up at the same time and did our Bible and devotional readings. She gave me a hug goodbye—ready to take on the day with all of her bags in hand—and started out the door for her shift. I heard the door open, but it shut right away, and she came back into the kitchen, setting everything back down on the island.

"Before I leave, can you tell me about the dream again?" She sat on the stool, hands folded, grinning ear to ear like a child about to receive the greatest present of all time.

We didn't have time for the whole story, so I started at the middle of the entry. She sat there soaking in every word, goosebumps forming on her arms, tears welling up in her eyes, but clearly enjoying every moment of it. Angie stared at the countertop as if she'd put herself in the dream. "I just can't believe how detailed it is! I can close my eyes, and it's like I'm right there with you."

Another moment of awkward silence passed before I hugged her goodbye. I grabbed my water and headed out to the patio to sit, listening to her car exit the driveway. I sat on the cushioned chair and watched the stillness of the lake, listening to the birds chirping ever so loudly.

It's just too real. Are you sure it was a dream? It couldn't have been, could it? You never dream, let alone something that real.

Throughout the day, I couldn't stop thinking about it. The more I reflected, the more I realized that my previous statement was false. I actually *had* dreams prior to this one. I dream all the time. They just don't occur in the night. I have dreams of being completely healed or winning a lottery I've never played. I have dreams of being a better daughter, friend, and sister. Dreams of reclaiming the title "daughter of Christ." I sat there in silence, thinking about all of my dreams and the fact that if I worked hard enough, they could be more than that.

I exited the patio, my feet touching the hot, dry grass. I walked out on the dock to take a seat. The water seemed very still that morning. In fact, it was so still that I could see each passing school of fish beneath the dock.

I often wonder what the life of a fish is like. I wonder what they think about, or how they don't worry about the hook that may get them later that day. How do they sleep when boats are coasting over them? I often wonder what *their* story is. Fish can't possibly have a story, can they? Why can't they? The truth is that everybody and everything has a story, and it's often one you know nothing about.

I stared at the bottom of the shallowest part of the lake. *This is actually happening! I never thought I'd see the day, but someday, somebody will want to hear the story. Amazing things are finally happening in your life, and someday, somebody is going to want to hear your story. The story of Kinze Berg.*

I started wrapping up the book of Exodus that morning. For those of you who aren't familiar with the book of Exodus, it's a great read! It's where we find the story of the ten plagues, the first Passover, the parting of the Red Sea, as well as the Ten Commandments. The book of Exodus is the incredible story of how God rescued all the children of Israel from Egypt, molded them, and formed a beautiful relationship with them.

I opened my Bible to Exodus chapter 33, which starts by describing God's frustration with the Israelites, and telling Moses that it was now his turn to lead the people.

OK, newsflash. Moses didn't want to lead the people! Why would he want to help such stubborn and undeserving people?

The chapter continues with Moses building a tabernacle, continuing to worship God, and eventually asking for God's help. God and Moses went way back. They had a beautiful relationship, and Moses desperately needed guidance during this time. He was in a time of needing to trust God.

Moses essentially asked God, "Why am I the one who has to lead them and deal with their stubborn behaviors when they're YOUR people?"

God said, "Yes, Moses, they are my people, but YOU have to lead them! You don't have to do it alone. I will be with you every step of the way."

Moses piped up, "Uggggggh . . . FINE! But you have to do something for me. Show me your glory!"

God looked at him with one eyebrow raised. "Nope. How about you just trust me? I can show you something, just not my face. It'll destroy you into a million little pieces. But I'll make you a deal. If you go to a narrowing in this rock, I'll show you myself from behind. You can see my back but not my face. Nobody can see my face. Deal?"

OK, you got me. Those weren't the exact words God and Moses used, but I like to picture it from this perspective.

As I sat on the dock, I took the time to soak up everything that I had just read. Prior to all of this, the only thing I knew about Moses was that he was put in the bullrush as a baby and that he was later a prophet and a leader who received the Ten Commandments from God. That's it.

What I know now is that my story is very similar to Moses's. I wanted to see God's glory, and just like in Exodus 33:11, I spoke with God face-to-face in this dream, even though I couldn't see his face. I couldn't see his face because it would destroy me, but I didn't have to see his face in order to trust him and have him work miracles in my life.

Just like Moses, God placed me on the rock so that just like the rest of the people, I could trust him to provide for my needs. He gave me hope and showed me what was behind him instead of showing me who he was physically. He showed me what he could do and who he was, all without showing me who he actually was. How incredible is our God? That same God that encountered Moses is the same exact God that you and I encounter every single day.

About two months later, a friend pulled into the driveway to pick me up for church. We hadn't known each other very long—at least not long enough to talk about anything other than how good the worship team had been sounding or how warm the temperature was going to get that week. We continued driving down the road when she popped the big question out of nowhere.

"So, tell me. What's your story?" she asked, turning down the radio.

"What makes you think I have a story?" I asked sarcastically, throwing in a slight laugh.

"Don't fool yourself, sweetheart. We all have one. So let's hear it." She laughed a bit harder.

The conversation isn't going to happen at a slumber party, Kinze. This is going to be uncomfortable, regardless, so just rip off the Band-Aid and get it over with.

I looked out the window, grinning ever so slightly in the passenger rearview mirror. "Well, it's going to sound crazy, but it's actually kind of a funny story. It all started with something called a dream."

Chapter 4

BE A CUPCAKE IN A WORLD OF DONUTS

Set your minds on things above, not on earthly things.

Colossians 3:2

"Wait! I'm coming, just hold on!" I skipped the last three steps and basically tore the closet door off the hinges. "Where are my sandals!?" I yelled out to the car full of people waiting for me.

"They're in the closet. Just hurry up. We need to go!" Mom shouted back into the house from inside the car.

I slammed the door and raced into the garage to slip on Dad's sandals. My toes hung off the front, and there was a solid two inches hanging off the back, but I didn't care. I jumped into the back seat, and down the road we went. To this day, I can't remember where exactly we ended up, but what I do know is that those sandals sucked! With every step, I either tripped or left a sandal behind. My feet started to burn. They ached. And I developed blisters on the sides of my feet from struggling so hard to keep them on. I know, I know. "You poor baby," right?

You're probably thinking the same thing everyone else did that day. *Well, smarty-pants, what did you expect? You're trying to keep a size 11 shoe on a size 9 foot. What did you think was going to happen?* My brain was obviously underdeveloped at this stage in my life because I apparently was expecting a lot more.

When we got home, I slammed open the car door, threw the sandals across the garage, and marched upstairs to throw my tantrum.

Reminiscing on that scenario, I realized that this exact situation was, unfortunately, pretty common in my life. In fact, I bet if you sit and ponder long enough, you too will realize that it's common in your own life. You maybe just don't recognize it yet. Whether it be throwing a tantrum or trying to fit a size 11 on a size 9, I'll leave that up to you to decide. Anyway, I didn't recognize that Dad's shoes were going to harm my feet. I just didn't want to be left behind.

That's always the case, isn't it? We just never want to be left behind. We always want what someone else has or want something that doesn't belong to us. When I ask you to think of a scenario similar to mine, I'm not asking you if you have ever or ever will physically put on someone else's shoes. Yes, I'm asking the question: When did you try to fit into someone else's shoes? But more importantly, I'm asking you: When did you stop wearing *your* shoes? When did you stop living *your* life and decide to live someone else's *for* someone else?"

It's not uncommon to feel out of place in this world we live in. It's not uncommon to scroll through Facebook and Instagram and think, *Wow! Look at them, they're so beautiful! Why can't I be that beautiful?*

Or,

I wish I was a part of their family. They're always so kind to each other and seem to have it all figured out.

Or,

How is she always so calm when her life is a complete mess? My life isn't even close to being as bad as hers. Why can't I be like that?

How many times a day do we forget who we are because we're too busy and distracted by those around us? Newsflash: too many times.

The cover is not always the book. Consider all the things you don't see, all the things you'll never know.

Although she may be beautiful and have all the name-brand clothing, it takes her layers of makeup to appear that way because she can't stand her natural look, and she's up to her waist in credit card debt.

They may appear to be a perfect family, but the wife and kids have hidden bruises because they forgot to haul the garbage or were three minutes past curfew.

Just because she seems put together doesn't mean she doesn't drown herself in sleeping pills at night to take away the pain. Or she turns the music up so loud on her way home from work so she can't hear herself scream as she drives down the road because she doesn't want to be alive anymore, yet she can't work up the courage to drive her car off the road.

The moral of my story is that we spend way too much time trying to keep a size 11 shoe on a size 9 foot. We spend too much time trying to be just like every other jelly-filled donut in the box when, in reality, we were created to be the cupcake that got thrown in with the donuts. I understand that this thought is extremely random but think about it. Have you ever heard someone complain when a cupcake accidentally gets thrown into their assortment of donuts? I certainly never have. In fact, I would probably be the one person in the group to say, "Heck yeah, a cupcake!"

Let's look at it from a different perspective. Let's say you work in an office, and everyone decides that being it's Friday, you should get Dairy Queen Dilly Bars. When you go inside to pick them out, are you going to ask for thirty cherry Dilly Bars? Chances are you're probably going to ask for ten cherry, ten chocolate, and ten butterscotch.

Why? Do you really think that among a group of thirty people, not one person will want a different flavor from somebody else? Do you think if you asked every person in your office what kind of Dilly Bar they wanted, they would all say cherry, or chocolate, or butterscotch? The odds of that happening are incredibly slim. It's slim because we aren't all alike, and we're not supposed to be. It's OK if you like cherry and I like butterscotch; it's not going to ruin our friendship. I promise.

If you can't tell by this point, I am a woman who loves analogies, or maybe it's my undiagnosed ADHD; I haven't figured it out yet. Analogies help me see a bigger picture so I can help *you* see a bigger picture. I want to help you see that you *deserve* to be a cupcake in a world of donuts. We all deserve to be a cupcake because of the glory and grace of God, who gave his only Son to die for you and me so that we could live the life that he created for us when he placed us in our mother's womb.

I know what you're probably thinking, *Kinze, the Bible doesn't say anything about cupcakes, or donuts, or scones, or anything of that nature. Nowhere in the Bible does it say that God created you to be a cupcake among the donuts.*

You're absolutely right! It wasn't put in so many words, but it does say in Romans 12:2, "Do not conform to the pattern of this world, but be transformed by the renewing of your mind. Then you will be able to test and approve what God's will is—his good, pleasing and perfect will," which is basically the same thing.

We weren't planted in our mother's womb to live a life like

Jack, or Lucy, or Mark, or Karen. He planted us in our mother's womb so that we were born to live a life through the eyes and heart of Christ. He planted us in our mother's womb exactly how he wanted us planted, and he knew us before we were even born. If you continue to wake up every morning thinking that God must have made a mistake when he created you, I want you to read these next lines over and over again until they're engraved into your brain.

God knows what he is doing! The Bible says in John 16:33, "I have told you these things, so that in me you may have peace. In this world you will have trouble. But take heart! I have overcome the world." Believe me, I have searched many different Bibles front to back, and I can promise you that nowhere does it say that our life is going to be easy. It doesn't say that we were going to have a "perfect" life like Jack or Lucy. But it *does* say exactly that you *will* have trials and sorrows, and you don't have to fear or be troubled because Jesus has overcome the world!

So why do you fear? Why do you say that he must have made a mistake? Why do you continue to compare, knowing that he created your life for *you* and their life for *them*?

I'm not saying that if you stop comparing yourself to others and walk in your own path, life is magically going to be filled with the fairytale story we all dream of. What I am saying is that God knows what he is doing. You just have to open your heart to him, and he will take care of the rest. But if you continue to wake up every morning bitter, resentful, and hateful toward the world and everyone in it, you're never going to see change. You're never going to see change unless you're willing to *make* the change, and the only change is him. I've lived my life with Jesus, and I've lived my life without Jesus, and I am living proof that life *with* Jesus is much better and a whole lot safer than without.

One of the most beautiful things in my career as a respiratory therapist is the number of believers I come across. They're struggling to breathe and sometimes need an assistive device to do so. But many times when I enter the room, a Bible is found in their hand, or they're partaking in the Sunday service available on the television, or they have the instrumental music channel on and are taking that time to pray. I love seeing that! These people are having the hardest days of their lives but continue to put their trust and faith in Jesus.

I was having a conversation with a patient recently who was going in for heart surgery that afternoon. Of course, he was nervous. The heart is a major organ; one wrong move and you're dead on the table. He was in chapter 3 of Ecclesiastes that morning and became emotional.

"Everything has its time. Today might just be mine," he said with tears in his eyes.

"Come on now, sir. You know as well as I do that today is not the day. You have the Word of God at your fingertips. There is no need to fear," I said as my voice broke.

"Ahhhh, so you know Jesus? Not many people do. They should, but they don't. Throughout my forty years as a pastor, my wife (since passed) and I have seen many come and go, so it's nice when to come in contact with people who believe," he said, scratching his beard and closing his Bible.

"I may have heard of him. He seems alright." I chuckled as I threw him a wink and a slight grin. I knew this gentleman had been a Christian for a long time. The pages were practically falling out of his Bible from being turned so many times, and the cover appeared worn and faded.

I realized at that moment that what I was saying probably didn't really matter. Maybe I provided comfort; maybe I just caused him more anxiety and distress. I had no idea. What I knew was the reality that not a single one of us knows when the Lord is going to call us home, so instead of continuing to waste my breath with words of encouragement, I took that moment to pray with this gentleman instead. I had been on his side of the fence, and in those moments of the unknown, I never wanted words of encouragement or somebody to tell me the odds. All I ever wanted was someone to grab my hand and do what I did with this man in his desperate time of need.

We finished praying, and there was a brief moment of silence.

"This will all be OK. I just gotta win the lottery," he chuckled.

The comment was a bit random and had nothing to do with what we were talking about—unless by lottery he meant surviving surgery—but I went along with it.

"Oh yeah? How long have you been playing?" I asked.

"Oh, sweetheart, I don't play."

If this guy was basing his chances of winning a lottery he never plays, it wasn't going to turn out well.

"Well, then it's a good thing you believe in God then, huh?" I asked.

There was a classmate I went to school with who used sports as an outlet. Many people have outlets (mine happened to be music). The first night of his senior basketball game, this kid went off on the coach in front of the entire gymnasium and stormed out. I later learned he thought that because he was a senior, he would get a starting position, and when he looked at the roster, his name wasn't listed. Nobody in the crowd knew what was happening, but the coach and his teammates definitely did.

The crowd didn't know that he'd missed every practice. Or that he had failing grades because drugs and alcohol took over his life. They didn't know he'd barely touched a basketball in two years.

He never put in the work but was mad at his teammate, who did *everything* to get that starting position.

How true is that for us and our journey with Christ? How many of us want all of God's glory or the benefits that come with being his child, but don't want to take the time to develop that intimate relationship with him? As I write this chapter, tears fill my eyes because part of me feels like an absolute hypocrite. Some of you will wonder as you read: *How can you sit there and write this when you turned away from him yourself? How about when you were that hostile person who wanted to throw the first stone? Now you're trying to come back and act like this saint, as if you've never done wrong in your life?*

Believe me, I agree. If I were reading this book, I'd have the same thoughts. But here's the truth: I've done wrong, and knowing me, I will probably do wrong in the future because guess what? I'm human. I've repented for the wrong that I have done, and I have and will give myself grace, now and in the future, just as he has given me.

Let's revisit the Gospel of John. If you have a Bible nearby, I want you to turn to chapters 7 and 8, where the scribes and the Pharisees bring a woman forth to be stoned for committing adultery. The Bible says:

> Jesus bent down and started to write on the ground with his finger.
>
> When they kept on questioning him, he straightened up and said to them, "Let any one of you who is without sin be the first to throw a stone at her."
>
> Again he stooped down and wrote on the ground.
>
> At this, those who heard began to go away one at a time, the older ones first, until only Jesus was left,

> with the woman still standing there. Jesus straightened up and asked her, "Woman, where are they? Has no one condemned you?"
>
> "No one, sir," she said.
>
> "Then neither do I condemn you," Jesus declared. "Go now and leave your life of sin." (John 7:7–11)

Just as Jesus saw the adulterous woman as human, so are we. More importantly, he sees us as sons and daughters of Christ. We have made and will make mistakes, but if we wake up each morning striving to be better than yesterday, through him, don't you consider that a win? I do! He does! As Christians, we find ourselves living in a world dominated by the attractiveness of materialism and self-indulgence and can oftentimes experience the feeling of being a misfit. But as a Christian, I believe that it's my duty to constantly strive to live a life of faith and humility amid the temptations and pressures of society.

Something I keep in mind often is that I cannot live a life of willful unforgiveness, resentfulness, and bitterness and expect to experience the blessings of God's goodness and grace. Let me ask you this: Do you reward a child who has thrown themselves onto the floor of the frozen treats aisle because you said no to the new Spiderman popsicles? Maybe you do, but most of us don't. The same goes for God; if I misbehave and am disrespectful toward him, he's not going to give me something just because I hurl myself on the floor and throw a tantrum. Believe me, I've tried.

I can, however, live a life full of the fruit of the holy spirit: "love, joy, peace, forbearance [patience], kindness, goodness, faithfulness, gentleness and self-control" (Galatians 5:22–23). And guess what? You can too! If we produce the fruit of the Spirit by remaining on the vine, and if we read Scripture and have a little talk with Jesus, he will make things right. Will we have days of resentfulness, bitterness, judgment, and lack of understanding or compassion? Absolutely. There will be times when it seems as if we're getting back into old habits and going down memory lane. But a wise friend once told me, "It's never too late to start again." And an even wiser friend often asks me, "Have you talked to Jesus about it yet?"

Start again, and please . . . talk to Jesus.

If you have to start over one hundred times, then start over one hundred times. Eventually, you will catch on. How many times does a baby learning to walk fall and get back up before they get the hang of it? Even when we're adults and have years of walking experience, does that mean we never trip over our feet again in our entire lifetime? I trip over my own feet at least thirty times a day—if that tells you anything. How many times does a child have to scrape the dirt off their knees and pick their bike up because they're not used to riding without training wheels? Once the training wheels are off, do we never wipe out again?

Someday, you will be able to ride without training wheels. You'll still wipe out every now and again, but at the end of the day, you still know how to ride the bike. Just because you wiped out this one time doesn't mean you totally forgot how to ride a bike. Pick it up, dust it off, and get back on.

The same goes for yourself. When you fall, get back up and return to what you know: you know what you're doing because God knows what *he* is doing.

We can only see the moment that we're in, but he has the bird's eye view. He knows what tomorrow holds, when to move us forward, and when to hold us back. And when we find ourselves stuck in that rut, we pray on that too. Lean on God and the people he has put into your life because they were placed there for a reason. Whether it be for a lifetime or just a season, he placed them in our lives because he knew that we needed them, or maybe it was that they needed us. Not using what God has given you is like being given the keys to the Batmobile and deciding to walk instead. Who does that?

If there is anything you can take away from this, let it be that God has not given up on you. Just because he is silent does not mean he has stopped working. Allow me to paint you a picture. At the age of eighteen, I bought some property near my parents with hopes to build on it one day. Seven years later, I'm finally finishing the process. Just because I didn't have the house up the first day I bought the land doesn't mean a house wasn't in the process. It took seven years, and lots of other obstacles and roadblocks along the way, to build up enough money to be able to go through with the house that I wanted to put on that property.

Now, I'm in another season of waiting. House projects are expensive and time-consuming. There's a different individual and specialist for every job. One day the plumber comes, the next day the electrician comes; the next day they have to do this, and the next day after that is something different, etc.

The home is being shipped from another part of the state. The process, unfortunately, doesn't happen overnight; it takes time to build it in a factory and time to get it here safely. Just as I've had to be patient and sit in seasons of waiting, you will also have seasons of waiting. But just because you are waiting doesn't mean nothing is happening.

Our Father is no different. He will put into our hearts the right thing to do in every situation, on *his* time, not ours. The hard thing is that if we become impatient and choose to go our own way because we think he's making a mistake, then he will let our circumstances and choices be our teacher! But if we are willing to surrender it all at his feet and say, "I don't know how you're going to do it, but I know you're going to do it," that's all he needs to hear, and he will take it from there.

Two words: *let him*. Two more words: *trust him*. Through every season in your life, God is preparing you for the next. Even though life sometimes feels chaotic and too overwhelming without direction, it's just God's path that you haven't realized you're on yet. It may seem as if other people are moving so much faster than you, but they are not. Either God is moving them in the right direction at the pace they need to go, or they're spiraling and doing self-directed things because they don't know Jesus and are completely lost.

Don't give up on him. He hasn't given up on you; he's just taking his sweet time to make you perfect in his image. If I've learned anything from this analogy, it's to stop following the ways of the world, start following the ways of my heavenly Father, and take a chance on being the cupcake in a world full of donuts.

Chapter 5

NIKKI FROM STARBUCKS

The LORD is close to the brokenhearted and saves those who are crushed in spirit.

Psalm 34:18

It's become a morning ritual to start my day at four o'clock in the morning, which has been a great addition to my daily routine and life. Have you ever been the first person up in your house? Or if you live alone, do you recognize how peaceful it is to be by yourself before you have to go into the chaotic environment called "the world"?

I've always been blessed with the ability to be both a morning person and a night owl. You need me up at 3:00 a.m.? Sounds good. I'll see you then! You need me to come pick you up at 23:00? I'm on my way. Maybe it comes from being a chronic insomniac who doesn't ever really sleep. Anyway, I have learned to enjoy being a morning person. There's something so peaceful and gratifying about being awake at four o'clock when the majority of people are still sleeping. Something so soothing and rewarding about being able to just be with myself and the Lord without interruption.

I was back at the cabin for a short stay, and this time, Angie and her husband were there with me. They've basically adopted me as another daughter at this point, so it's official: they're stuck with me. Angie happened to be working that weekend, so we were all up very early in the morning.

"I'm going to get up tomorrow morning and just head out when Angie does," I said.

"You're going to go home first at that hour? You don't have to leave; just stay here." They both looked at me with confused looks on their faces.

"No, I just have this feeling that I'm supposed to break my fast with Starbucks. It's been a while, so I think I'll treat myself." I chuckled.

During that time at the cabin, I chose to enter a three-day water fast. Before you ask, "Are you crazy?" let me say that I am already well aware and receiving proper treatment. Obviously, I'm kidding. Maybe. I will talk about it in a later chapter (the water fast, not being crazy. Well, that too, I suppose.). I decided to reward myself with the *fancy* coffee that morning—instead of my normal straight black—and finish my readings there instead of at the cabin.

I pulled out of the driveway, but as I drove down the road, I started to kick myself. *Why do you think you need a seven-dollar coffee? There was coffee and a beautiful view at the cabin. You should have just stayed there. You're already spending enough money on this house project. You're on a first-name basis with the UPS delivery driver, and now this?* I turned up the radio a little louder as if it was going to drown out the voices in my head.

Finally, after about five miles down the road, I pulled off to the side and looked at myself in the rearview mirror. *Kinze, this behavior has to stop. You're turning your reward into a negative situation, and it stops now. It's a seven-dollar coffee, not a seven-hundred-dollar purchase. Now, drive.*

I eased back onto the road, cranked the music, and pulled into the Starbucks parking lot not long after. But today felt different. I'd been to this Starbucks a few times but was not on a first-name basis with the barista like back when I was in college. There was nobody standing at the register asking me if I was going to take "the usual," so I decided that today was going to be the day I asked for something different. If you've never tried the cinnamon dolce latte at Starbucks, I recommend that you put this book down immediately and go and get yourself one; you won't regret it, and yes, it's worth the $7.

I sat down at the table farthest away from the entrance. I took my books and journals out, popped in my earbuds, and before I knew it, I had killed a couple of hours. I looked down at my watch only to realize that I still had plenty of extra time before church. I closed my books but kept my earbuds in as I finished my coffee while observing the environment around me. As I watched the baristas make drink after drink, I saw the door almost fly off the hinges out of the corner of my eye.

She didn't appear much older than me, stood about five-foot-five, and had a sweatshirt that went down to her knees. Her hair looked as if it hadn't been combed for days, and I could see mascara stains on the inner left sleeve and down her cheeks. She stood at the register, hot and bothered, and couldn't stand still to save her life. She began to rap her order to the poor teenager at the front, who looked as though it was her first day on the job. This girl didn't look like a chai tea type of girl, but instead, an "I'll take a grande ___, half almond half oat milk, three pumps of ________, half shot of ______, quad espresso" type of girl.

I shut off my phone and removed my earbuds one at a time.

"I'm sorry, you wanted three pumps of what?" the barista asked nervously.

"It's not that hard of an order!" the young girl screamed.

Thankfully, the manager stepped in and resolved the confusion with the touch of a button. I remain seated in the booth, silent but concerned. Normally, when I see these types of situations, my first thought is, "Can we get this girl a padded room?" But today was different. I wasn't nervous. I wasn't bothered. I was concerned. I started to pack up, and I looked at my journal cover. Engraved on the front in purple stitching is Psalm 46:10, "Be still and know that I am God."

I took my last sip of coffee and, in my head, asked, *Who hurt you? God, who hurt her?* You may be asking, "How do you know she was hurt? Maybe she was just having a tough day." Here's the thing: this wasn't a look of "I just broke up with my boyfriend" or "I just had a fight with my best friend." This was a look of desperation.

How do I know? Because not only do "hurt people hurt people," but hurt people recognize hurt people. Although I've never blown up at a barista, I have blown up at other people as a result of how I was feeling. So to say I was brought back to that moment in my life would be an understatement.

The young girl paced back and forth about thirty times before getting her drink. I thought she was going to sprint out the door, but much to my surprise she took a seat three tables down. My knee began to bounce, and I looked up, thinking, *Are you serious right now, is this why I'm here?*

My very short conversation with God was interrupted by the slamming of her phone on the table. I slowly turned my head to the left, praying I didn't get caught staring. She buried her head in her hands, sobbing.

She tried hard to hide it, but I could see the hiccupping of her belly and chest through the oversized sweatshirt. *Fine.* I shoved my books back in my bag, threw my cup in the garbage, and slowly approached this hurting soul. I invited myself to the chair across from her. I didn't know where to start, so I started with "How can I help?" I swallowed past the lump in my throat.

Smooth introduction, Berg, real smooth.

Her mascara continued to build on her sleeve. "I'm fine, thanks. Just having a moment. You wouldn't understand," she said, trying to cover up the blotches scattered across her face.

Before you give me the "I told you so" speech, just trust me when I say that it was more than "just having a moment," and she was far from "fine."

Well, God, there ya have it. She's fine. I'm going to go now.

I could hear him laugh . . . *Nice try.*

I have never really been a conversationalist. Those who know me really well will say that's hard to believe, but I always find myself struggling to find the right words to say. I'm awkward, and if you ask me to talk to someone who isn't a patient of mine or someone I'm not close with, then be prepared to watch a trainwreck. I sat there for a brief moment, cautiously choosing the words that were about to come from my mouth.

"You're right, but here's what I do understand. I understand that you're hurting, and although I may not know how you feel or how you're hurting, I know how *it* feels." Her head stayed pointed down, but her eyes raised up to meet mine.

She leaned against the back of the booth and crossed her arms. "Let me guess. You're either a shrink or a Bible thumper?"

I didn't feel that this was a moment I could release a laugh, so I copied her actions. I leaned against the back of my chair, crossed *my* arms, and said, "Close. I'm a respiratory therapist by trade, but most importantly, I am a child of God, yes."

She moved to stand up.

"Wait. Please don't go, not like this. I'm not here to shove a Bible down your throat. I just want to help. Can I at least get your name?" My anxiety started building.

Her jaw clenched, and I was uncertain as to whether or not I might receive five fingers to the face; or at least one. "Nikki."

I contemplated my next move. "OK, Nikki, don't run. But while we're on the subject, what is your relationship with God?"

She slowly peeled her thighs from the seat for the second time in five minutes. "I'll give it to you; you're persistent."

If looks could kill, I would have been dead right then and there. "It's just a question. Nothing more than just a girl trying to make conversation with a stranger."

She glared at me and slid back into the middle of the booth.

"This has got to be the worst blind date I've ever been on," I joked as I wiped the sweat from my palms, questioning every life decision I've ever made.

She clasped her hands around her cup, fingers still mildly trembling. "Methodist. Left the church at fourteen. Only went to please my mom. I started hanging out with the wrong group, got into drugs and alcohol, and went to jail at eighteen for covering for my boyfriend. I was supposed to serve fifteen years for a meth bust gone bad. Got out after three because he confessed, and my family said they wouldn't take me back. My brother talked to me, but he died in an accident a few years back. I lost my mom about six months ago, and now I don't know what to do, so I'm sitting here talking to you. How's that?"

One question opened up a whole can of worms. I stared at her blankly, but in my head said, *Lord help!* I was speechless. I honestly didn't know how to respond, and my heart broke for this girl even more the longer I listened to her speak.

"That's what I thought, but good luck with the next one," she said, starting to move her bag out of the booth.

"Nikki, wait, please. Let's just take a breath here." My voice broke, and I felt a tear form in my eyes. This time, she was actually going to leave.

"You can't help me. I've tried everything. It's just me, and I can't anymore. I'm sorry," she whispered.

I grabbed the sleeve of her hoodie. *Lord help me, I'm going to be sent to jail for harassment in a public place,* I thought as I took the deepest breath of my life. But here's the thing: she stopped. She didn't pull away.

Stay calm, stay calm, stay calm.

I stared at the empty seat across from me. "One more question. Why did you come here today?"

There was a brief moment of silence throughout the whole coffee shop—as if someone hit the pause button.

I heard what sounded like a little kid hyperventilating when they cry, that little hiccupping noise they make when they can't seem to catch their breath in between words. The hand that grabbed her sweatshirt was now resting back on my lap as Nikki sat back down for the one-hundredth time. I stared at the rise and fall of her chest, each breath becoming a little calmer.

She played with the tassels on her sweatshirt. "I didn't want to come. I just didn't know where else to go, and I thought coming here would help. I thought if I just got my favorite coffee that I'd be OK, and I'd be able to work through it."

I couldn't—but yet I could—believe what I was hearing. "Me neither," I said as a confused look came upon her face. "I didn't actually want to come here this morning either."

She looked at me as if I had two heads. "If you didn't want to come, then why are you here?"

A tear fell from my right eye as I grinned ever so slightly. "I think I'm looking at her." I explained my encounter with the Lord during my fast, my Saturday night thoughts, my drive that morning, and the talk I had to have with myself just to convince myself it was OK to go.

"You're not going to give it up, are you?" she asked, shaking her head.

"Umm, nope, I'm not. This whole encounter happened for a reason." I shifted in my seat.

"Yeah, it's called a coincidence." She laughed hard enough to make the barista shoot her a look.

I shook my head and smiled in disbelief. How could she even still believe in coincidences at this point? "I used to believe in those. Now I believe in something else."

"Oh yeah?" she asked. "And what's that?"

"Alignment," I said, not missing a beat.

In a matter of minutes, I was looking at a completely different person. She took a sip of coffee, and a blank stare came across her face. I wondered what she was thinking but decided to let her have a moment to think for once. After a few too many minutes passed by, I decided, once again, to open my big fat mouth.

"You can deny it, but in my heart, I know that something happened here today, and I know you believe that too. If you didn't, you would have run out as soon as I sat down." I sipped my second cup of coffee ever so slowly.

"I tried, but you wouldn't let me." An annoyed look came across her face as she threw her hands in the air.

"Well, did I hold you at gunpoint?" I laughed.

"OK. My turn. There has to be a reason why you're so persistent. A reason why you're so passionate yet extremely annoying." She tapped her fingers on the table.

"Am I getting somewhere?" I asked, trying not to be offended that I was just called annoying by a stranger.

Before I knew it, I was sharing bits and pieces of my story, and she was sharing parts of hers. As I spoke, something beautiful happened. Nikki no longer appeared uncomfortable, and she no longer seemed like a stranger but a close friend. In fact, it's almost as if she was never the blubbering mess that took the hinges off the door when she came in.

"I don't know. I just don't know." She got quiet again.

"You're not going to know what you don't know. That's the beauty of recreating yourself. What you've been through—the tragedy, the trauma—is *not* your identity. And now it's time to end this chapter and write a new one. And if you have to, just write an entirely different book. Recreate yourself. Rebuild your temple. Do whatever you have to do. Just know that this is not an ending but a beginning," I said, reaching across the table to hold her hand.

I didn't think there was any more mascara to wipe away or any room left on the sleeve, but I was wrong. She took time to think about her next actions.

"You're probably not going to believe this, but I didn't like you at first. And I didn't just come here for a coffee. I came here to create the plan," she said, wiping another tear.

I felt my lip start to quiver. "I know. But deep down you knew it couldn't be the end, so you came here. I know." I paused for a second. I knew that what was about to come out of my mouth next was probably going to be the one thing that sent her flying out the door.

"What if I told you that you could change, big or small, in three days? Heck, you could even see a little change in just one day, or even half a day."

She squinted her eyes ever so slightly. "I'd return back to my original thought that you're a Bible-thumping crazy person."

Again, trying not to be offended, I said, "I'll take it. I'm going to challenge you. Three days. Just give me three days. Go to your favorite place, near or far. If you don't have one, find one. Three days with no contact with the outside world. Bring a Bible. You don't even have to open it. Bring a journal, some music, a book—just try it for three days. I will say there will be more progress and better results if you recreate your relationship or, if you've never actually had one, *start* a relationship with God.

"My heart is telling me that something beautiful will happen when you do it, but *you* have to be the one to initiate it. I can't do it for you. Nobody can, not even God. It's a hard and really painful process, especially when you've lived in the same fishbowl for how many years, but I promise it'll be worth it. He seems silent now, and he will many times. But I promise that if you let him in, he will work in silence, and your life is going to change in ways you didn't even know were possible.

"There are going to be days where the highs feel high, and the lows feel low. The highs are always easy, but it's in the lows where you have to keep the faith. Just like riding a bike without training wheels, it'll take a while to get the hang of it, but it will come. I myself am still learning, but the transformation so far has been incredible!"

We both stood up to leave this time. "Would it be weird if I asked to hug you?" she asked sheepishly.

I busted a gut laughing. "Are you serious right now? After all of this, it would be weird, and I would be highly offended if you didn't!"

I grabbed her and pulled her in tighter than I have with any other individual in my entire life. For those of you who have ever had what friends call a "Kinze hug," you are probably finding this very hard to believe. About a minute passed by, and it was almost as if Nikki had become limp.

Did she pass out? Did I go too far? I lifted my head, and she slowly pulled away.

With tears in her eyes, she took a slow, deep breath. "The last person I hugged was my brother . . . So thank you for this."

I got into my car and sat there praying for about fifteen minutes before pulling out of the parking lot to go to church. About one minute down the road, I screamed a choice word that I will not reveal. *I didn't get her number.* I pulled into the church parking lot and started to cry. *How could you not have exchanged information? YOU'RE SUCH AN IDIOT!*

As I waited for the tears to dry and the swelling underneath my eyes to disappear, I remembered Acts 1:7. "It is not for you to know the times or dates the Father has set by his own authority." I wiped my eyes, took a drink of water, and slammed the car door.

You're right. Take it from here, Big Guy.

I entered the church and was immediately greeted by Pastor Char. "Kinze! Hi, good to see you! How was your week?"

I still hadn't wrapped my head around what had just happened moments before. I hesitated but eventually was able to say, "Week was good, but I just got called a crazy Bible thumper."

Out of everything you could have told her about the encounter, that was what you could come up with? Seriously? I tried to change the wording, but I couldn't think of the right words to say except, "I can't wait to tell you about it."

I sat in my usual spot, feeling the adrenaline move from the top of my head to the soles of my feet. People of the church were coming up to talk to me, but all I could see was their lips moving. I wasn't actually listening. All I could think about at that moment was Nikki from Starbucks, and how I could find her again? *I know it's not my job to know, God, but I have to! I have to know what happens to her!* It was as if I was anticipating what was going to happen on the next episode of one of Netflix's finest.

I sat in silence before the lights went dim and the worship team began to sing "Great Are You Lord." The words hit my heart as if I hadn't listened to the song a billion times. My extremities were pale and cold, but I had a warm feeling in my heart. It felt strange yet comforting at the same time. The tears rolled down my cheek, and to save myself from embarrassment, I buried my head in my hands. Then a gentle hand touched my right shoulder.

"How can I pray for you?" she asked.

I stared at her for some time before choking up, saying, "Actually I don't want you to pray for me. Is that OK?"

She looked at me with an offended look, but I explained myself before she had time to walk away. "I don't want you to pray *for* me. I want you to pray *with* me. I want to pray for the healing of Nikki from Starbucks. She's a young girl that I met this morning, and to keep a long story short, she's really struggling and needs to find Jesus."

This lady put her arm around my left shoulder and placed her head on my right. "Lord, we come before you tonight in prayer. I don't know the entire story, but you and Kinze do, and that's all you need. Lord, we come before you tonight to ask for strength and healing, not just for Nikki but for all those who are in need of your healing power and presence. Thank you, Lord, for your great blessings, for your mercy, for your grace, and for the work that is about to be done for Nikki and all those who are lost in the world right now. In Jesus's name, amen."

Chapter 6
DEVIL'S FOOD

Therefore, my dear brothers and sisters, stand firm. Let nothing move you. Always give yourselves fully to the work of the Lord, because you know that your labor in the Lord is not in vain.

1 Corinthians 15:58

2 cups all-purpose flour
2 teaspoons baking soda
1 teaspoon salt
½ teaspoon baking powder
½ cup unsalted butter
1 cup Dutch-processed cocoa powder (sifted)
½ cup vegetable oil
1 ½ cups granulated sugar
½ cup packed brown sugar
3 large eggs
1 tablespoon vanilla extract
½ cup sour cream
1 cup milk
1 cup hot coffee

Shoot, this was supposed to go in my recipe book![4] Sorry guys! Well, while we're here, let's just roll with it, shall we? I love a good devil's food cake. Isn't the saying, "It's so good it has to be sinful?" I turned on the television one morning, and the chocolate cake scene from *Matilda* appeared across the screen. I used to love that movie as a child, but have you ever watched it as an adult? I was sitting on the couch, and I could feel the disgusted look on my face. *How can he eat so much cake? If I ate that much, I'd need a five-gallon pail to throw it back up in.*

As he continues eating, the character begins to enter a "sugar coma," and Matilda is the first to stand up and begin cheering him on. "Come on, Bruce! You can do it!" Soon the entire school starts cheering him on: "BRUCE! BRUCE! BRUCE! BRUCE!"[5]

Just like Bruce overindulged, how many times do we overindulge in our lifetime? How many times do we overindulge in a single day? Maybe you sat down with the pint of mint chocolate chip ice cream and finished the entire thing in one sitting. Maybe you said you were only going to have two slices of pizza but, instead, finished off the entire sixteen-inch yourself. Or maybe you decided you could fit a week's worth of activities into one day, and now you're sitting there scratching your head, wondering why you're feeling burned out.

How many times do we overindulge and not even realize it? How many times do we enter that "coma," becoming so tired we can barely function, yet the devil cheers us on while God shouts, "STOP! You're doing too much!"

How many times are we fueled by the devil, but when God shouts for us to stop and rest, we completely ignore him? Why don't we ignore the devil instead? Proverbs 4:23 says "Above all else, guard your heart, for everything you do flows from it." What does it look like for you to guard your heart?

I won't lie to you. There was a moment in my life when I thought "guarding my heart" meant putting up a wall. Nothing comes in; nothing goes out. It meant if you don't let them in, they can't hurt you.

Guarding my heart meant doing everything to not stick out like a sore thumb or to show anyone that I was in excruciating pain. But over time, I began to un-guard my heart. I began to overindulge in habits such as late-night parties, gummies of non-Haribo sorts, drinking straight out of the vodka bottle, and lying to people about where I was or what I was doing. This wasn't me; this was who the devil wanted me to be.

"Come on, Kinze! Life is short. Live it while you're still here! Come on. It's just one night! It's just one drink. It's just one gummy. It's just one pill!" The devil cheered me on, and I let him get into my mind, heart, body, and soul.

He completely took over, and I soon became someone that some people hardly recognized. I stopped communicating with certain friends, some labeling me as "cold and calloused." I drank until I had the bed spins and couldn't even stand on my own two feet. I'd say I was going to a friend's house for the night as I snuck out with a boy from the online dating app or decided to go out on the town with a group of strangers.

Was I happy? Of course not! I had been to hell and back time and time again but had never felt as miserable as I did in these moments.

I woke up one morning, PJ (Pre Jesus), and I didn't even recognize myself. Through my bloodshot eyes and pale complexion, I said, "Come on, Kinze, I know you're in there. You're better than this. Please, stop doing this." I sat on the couch and looked at my phone as I contemplated sending the message. I must have re-read it a million times before clicking send: "Hi Jennifer, it's Kinze. Are you still doing therapy, and if so, may I schedule an appointment?"

For the past five years, I had stopped and started therapy at least a dozen times. I expected to look at my phone and see: "Sorry, kid. You're too far gone. I can't help you. But good luck!"

Before I could even set the phone down, I had a response back. "Hi Kinze. Yes, I'm still doing sessions. Would this day and time work for you?"

I took a deep breath as I typed, "See you then! Can't wait!"

Seriously? Can't wait? For therapy? Yeah, that's believable.

I sat and stared into my empty coffee cup. "Are you sure you want to do this?" asked the voice in my head. You have no idea how many times I went back and forth with it before I lost it. Thank goodness nobody was home because I had a mess to clean up. I threw the cup into the sink, and it shattered everywhere. I began to cry and punched the counter so hard I thought I broke my knuckles. *I have to do something, or I'm not going to be alive much longer.*

At this point in my medical journey, I wasn't sure I was going to be alive much longer anyway, but by doing what I was doing, I was going to have one foot in the grave by evening. I got ready for the day, grabbed my journal, and began to start making a list of everything that had gone on since my last counseling session. Newsflash: it was a lot!

I pulled into the parking lot and began to have a pre-therapy panic attack. *Kinze, it's fine. You're fine. Get it together!* I chugged my bottle of water and started walking up the steps to where I was greeted by the bench. "Benchie" and I go back. We've cried together. We've laughed together. I've fainted on him a few times; we have history.

"Hello, buddy ol' pal. Long time no see," I said as I sat down to collect my thoughts.

"Back for more, eh? How long before you quit this time?" I imagined him saying, as I wiped the sweat from my palms, waiting for her door to open. A few minutes later, I sat on her couch, looking like a puppy waiting to be chosen at the pound.

"Thank you so much for seeing me. Again. I didn't think you would take me back (as if I were some orphan child) after I started and stopped so many times. Thank you. I really appreciate it." I tried to hold the vomit inside as I conversed with her.

I left my "first" session and knew that there was a lot of work that needed to be done. After all, it wasn't my first rodeo. *If only I could break myself down completely and build myself back up. If only I could destroy this body and just get a new one.* As I drove home that day, I thought about all the people in my life who did the "Hokey Pokey" and turned themselves around. There are thousands of people every day who decide to break a habit, take on a new hobby, or reconstruct their lives. Some people even go as far as moving to a new state and changing their name, which believe me, I had already considered at this stage, but it seemed a little extreme.

It wasn't long after this "first" session that I was at the cabin with Angie getting a tour and having my quarter-life crisis. It wasn't long after this that I decided to open my heart back up to Christ. It wasn't long after that I made the decision to do some soul searching and reinvent myself.

I had been to church with Angie twice before the cabin experience. I wasn't fully sold, nor was my heart entirely open to the idea of accepting Christ back into my life. I had felt let down by him so many times and had started to believe he wasn't anything more than a cartoon character at this point. It wasn't until I was on the cabin doorstep, *desperate* for anyone or anything to take this pain away from me. It wasn't until I cried out to him that he said, "FINALLY! Was that so hard? All you had to do was ask!" It's kind of humorous looking back on the moment, but it was not one bit funny in the actual moment.

I had thought that there had been many times when I hit rock bottom in my life. But let me tell you, you haven't hit rock bottom until the only thing left to do is fall flat on your face and knees and beg, "PLEASE, GOD! *Please*!" You haven't hit rock bottom until you have had to completely give up your pride—and everything else in your life—and humble yourself to the One and Only. If you're reading this thinking, "That'll never be me," just know that we were once in the same boat.

Fast forwarding a few months, I was at my all-time high. My color was better. I had more energy, was tolerating solid food, was sleeping great, and then I hit a low. It's true what they say: "When you're high, you're high; when you're low, you're low." I wasn't at the lowest point in my life, but I recognized I was starting to go down some paths I swore I was never going to go down again. I continued to read the Bible, pray, and go to church, but I felt like the flame wasn't as bright.

I was at church one Saturday evening, sitting in my usual spot. *Lord, I don't understand. I'm doing everything I'm supposed to be doing. Why am I at the wall again? I feel like I'm losing sight of you all over again. Please, Lord! I'll do better. I'll do more. I'll give more!* It was at this moment that I needed my own advice: just because he is silent doesn't mean he has stopped working. The truth is that sometimes walls aren't meant to be a roadblock but, instead, something to rest and lean against for a while. And in my case, I was in desperate need of a rest.

I was in this rut for about a week, maybe a little longer, and I could feel myself starting to become frustrated. But even though I was frustrated, I kept my promise to remain faithful to God as he remained faithful to me.

I went to bed one night and couldn't fall asleep. I tossed and turned, prayed, counted sheep, and even took sleep medication. I tried everything, and yes, I even read scripture. I picked up my tablet, popped in my earbuds, and started scrolling through YouTube. As I scrolled, I saw the photo to the left of the video on fasting. I had tried intermittent fasting in the past and wasn't really a fan. But this wasn't just a video on fasting. This was one on biblical fasting. The video was thirty-seven minutes long (I know, oddly specific), so I didn't click on it. But I knew what I planned to do that following morning: research biblical fasting.

Fasting is found multiple times throughout the Bible and is something practiced all over the world by people of many different faiths. Often, fasting is performed not for just spiritual benefits but for physical benefits, and most individuals who participate in fasting don't even know Jesus. Not only does fasting have a great deal of physical health benefits, but it also has many spiritual health benefits as well. As you read the Bible, you will find many different types and lengths of fasts and will learn how they have changed lives in just a short amount of time.

In Judges 20:26, there was a fast from sunrise to sunset to seek direction from the Lord. In Acts 9:9, Saul did a three-day fast for conversion. The Daniel fast, found in Daniel 10:3, is a very common twenty-one-day fast done throughout many churches, often in times of distress and mourning. Jesus even went as far as doing a forty-day fast (Matthew 4:1–11). Whether someone chooses to do a one-day or forty-day fast, one is just as powerful as the other as long as they keep a godly heart and attitude.

Again, you're probably asking, "Are you crazy?" to which I'll respond again, "Yes, but I'm receiving proper treatment."

I've had to fast in the past, and with my gastrointestinal history it's nothing for me to do a week's worth of water fasting. I went back to the cabin that week with the mindset: "Three days? This is going to be a walk in the park."

I woke up that first morning ready to kick it into gear! I grabbed my gallon water bottle and took the first chug. I immediately got nauseated and began to regret my decision. *Nope. Once you're in, you're in. Sorry pal.*

I took another chug. *OK, that was better.*

Another chug. *Nope! What the heck is your deal? You love water; you drink it all the time!* I set the water bottle down and walked out to the patio.

I stared at the lake, then turned around to see my reflection in the window. A cold chill went down my spine, and I felt as if I were looking Satan straight in the eyes. *Nice try, but it ain't gonna work. I'm doing this!*

The experience made me realize this fast was actually much different than what I've had to do in the past. Yes, I've fasted for lengthy amounts of time, but I *had* to for medical reasons. In those moments of fasting, I was really sick, so it was nothing for me to not eat because I didn't feel like it anyway. And what happened during some of those times? My body was able to heal on its own without surgical intervention!

This time, however, I *could* eat, and that's why this was so hard. My body was craving food. The *devil* was craving food, and he wasn't getting any, so he was throwing his tantrum by trying to play his tricks.

The physical benefits of fasting are amazing, according to the research I found, but the body undergoes a lot of stress during this process. After about twelve hours on a water fast, your body enters ketosis, which is basically where the body begins to eat its own fat, being it can't rely on food. After about one to two days, your body goes from ketosis to autophagy, which is where your body basically begins to eat itself.[6]

It sounds like a disgusting process, but it's actually quite incredible. It's amazing that God created our bodies so that when we fast, there's a process that occurs where the body eats damaged cells so it can generate new ones.

You'll want to do the research yourself and consult your own medical professional, but here's what I took from my study: Want a new body? Fast. Want to see physical and spiritual changes in your life? Fast. Of course, people with medical conditions should consult a physician before doing so, or if they have to, minimize it as much as they can. Again, all types of fasts are just as powerful as the next, as long as someone has the right heart and mindset.[7]

I don't know what I was expecting when I made the decision to do this, but what I do know is that what occurred during this time definitely exceeded *any* expectations I had. The biggest lesson I learned was that powerful breakthroughs happened when I denied my body of physical needs like food and started shifting my mind to rely on what my body spiritually needed. I thought going into this that I had an incredible amount of self-control, but I was wrong. I had a long way to go, and this really brought that to light.

Post fast, I have more self-control than I have ever had in my entire life. It's not perfect, but I'm better than I was before, and that's all anyone can ask for.

Let me ask you this: How many times do you open the kitchen cupboards when you're at home by yourself with nothing to do? Is it because you're hungry or because you're bored? For me, 99.9 percent of the time it's because I'm bored. Do you know how hard it is to be locked up in a cabin with nothing to do, surrounded by food, knowing that you can't have any of it?

The answer is: *hard*, especially on day one. It got easier, though, because I had the Word of God to lean on! When I entered a time of biblical fasting, it forced me to seek his face and lean into him for help. I fasted to show and prove to God that my hunger for him far surpasses my hunger for anything else.

If you've found yourself hitting a roadblock, I'm not saying, "Just go fast for a few days, and it will all be fine." I would love for that to be the case, but there's more to it. You have to first open your heart and mind to the idea that you are the only person on this planet who can change your life. You are the only person who can guard your heart, and by that, I mean only *you* can control what flows in and out of it.

Guarding your heart is not putting a cement wall around your heart and becoming cold. Instead, it means that you're going to wake up and realize: *I recognize that this is happening, but I'm not going to let it affect who I am as a person.* It's being able to recognize: *I feel angry, but I am not an angry person.* It's being able to admit to God: *I'm not sure what your plan is, but I know it's going to be greater than what I could ever do on my own.* It's waking up each morning craving *angel* food, not *devil's* food!

Chapter 7
IT DOESN'T HAVE TO BE THIS WAY

Blessed is the one who perseveres under trial because, having stood the test, that person will receive the crown of life that the Lord has promised to those who love him.

James 1:12

My grandma used to babysit a few boys who lived in town when I was in elementary school. Have you ever watched somebody do something and wonder how they do it all and make it look so easy? She was always such a natural—a natural caretaker, a natural cook, a natural baker, a natural woman. It didn't matter what she did in life; she always made it seem so easy. Thankfully, I was not only blessed to call her Grandma, but I was blessed to also call her daughter Mom. Growing up, it was always my number one goal in life to be just like them.

One day, Grandma was babysitting the boys, and for the first time ever in my life, she snapped at me. I was about nine years old at the time but old enough to know better. I never heard my grandma yell, and if I did, it was never at me.

I began to bawl my eyes out, and as I ran down the stairs to the garage, I looked back and screamed, "I hate you! You're the WORST grandma ever! I HATE YOU!"

The next morning, Mom was sitting at the kitchen table on the phone with Grandpa. "I don't know. She got really sick yesterday afternoon, and it got worse overnight. They're taking her to Saint Mary's in Rochester."

I knew it was bad because Mom sat there empty-handed—no breakfast, no coffee, no newspaper, nothing.

My grandma was a diabetic, and she came down with a condition called pancreatitis. It was one of the worst cases the doctors had ever seen. Pancreatitis is an inflammation of the pancreas that occurs when certain proteins or enzymes begin to work in your digestive tract while still in the pancreas.[8] In Grandma's case, it began to shut down not only her pancreas but her entire body as well. She lost her ability to breathe on her own and was placed in a medically induced coma, on a ventilator, so that her body could heal.

For about a month, we drove back and forth to Rochester every single day. One day, we showed up, and although her hospital bracelet and whiteboard said "Donna Shogren," she looked absolutely nothing like herself. The medications they had been pumping into her bloodstream made her look unrecognizable.

"That's not Grandma," I said, looking up at Grandpa.

"Yes, it is, sweetie. She's just sick right now," he said as he held back the tears.

We went back to the waiting room, and I continued playing my game on the computer. That's what they do with kids in these situations. They stick you in front of a computer or throw a book at you and basically say, "Here kiddo. Do this to distract yourself from the fact that the woman you love more than anything in this world is dying." I played along with their games, but I wasn't stupid. I knew what was happening. I may not have understood all the medical terminology at that age, but when a nine-year-old walks into a hospital room and sees what I saw that day, you know it's not good. We went down to the cafeteria for lunch—not that we were ever actually hungry—and when we got back, I saw the doctor pull Mom and Grandpa aside.

"It's in God's hands now." I couldn't hear the full conversation, but I know what I heard.

If you've never been to Saint Mary's Hospital, consider yourself one lucky individual. If you want to see a beautiful cathedral, I recommend going just for that experience. But otherwise, congratulations on not being one of "the chosen ones." I've only set foot in that cathedral once since 2007, and although it's beautiful, I think it will be quite some time before I enter it again. The cathedral is where many people not only go to pray but to mourn. Every time we went to pray, I couldn't. I was too distracted by the wails and screams from those asking God the dreaded question: *Why?*

I remember the moment as if it were yesterday. The afternoon of August 28, 2007, we were sitting in the back pew on the left-hand side. There was a young woman and a child sitting in the front pew on the right-hand side, and she was cradling her child as if he was a newborn baby, and there wasn't a single tear left to shed. I couldn't stop staring, not because I was judging, but because in my head and in my heart, I thought, *That's going to be me, isn't it?*

Grandpa put the kneeler down, made the sign of the cross, closed his eyes, and folded his hands (it's a pretty common sequence, especially in the Catholic faith). Have you ever watched somebody pray and wondered what they prayed about? *What does a prayer look like to them?* Growing up in the Catholic church, it's actually very unfortunate that they don't teach you how to pray. It's possible that I missed that Wednesday night class, but I went to Catechism for nine years and never remembered the lecture on prayer or the importance thereof. Perhaps you're reading this and asking, "What the heck are you even talking about?! They teach you how to pray!"

Of course, Catholics know and are taught how to pray, but how many Catholics can pray from their heart and not just recite the "Our Father," or "Hail Mary," or "Act of Contrition," or "The Rosary"? Yes, those are just as important, but how many Catholics (or even non-Catholics) could place their hands on a hurting (or non-hurting) individual and actually pray for them? I'm not saying it doesn't happen; I'm just saying I wasn't one of the fortunate ones to learn how at that time.

Grandpa was deep in prayer, but if I wanted to see God work, I had to know what to do.

I leaned in really close and whispered in his ear. "Grandpa? How do you pray?"

He sat back in the pew, put the kneeler up, and wrapped his arms around me. "Well, kiddo, just pretend that you're talking with a friend. It's kind of like when we take you to see Santa (Yes, I still believed in Santa at the age of nine, and still do at the age of twenty-five, so mind your business). You go up to him, you thank him, you tell him how good you've been, and then you tell him everything you're wishing for. And if he feels it in his heart that this year is the right year for you to receive that gift, he will put it under the tree. Understand?"

I thought about what he had said, and I began to pull the kneeler back down. *OK. Just like Santa. . . . In the name of the Father, Son, Holy Spirit. Close your eyes. . . . Fold your hands. . . . Jesus? Thank you. I think I've been a good girl this year. Please make Grandma better. I'm sorry for what I said. I didn't mean it. She's the BEST grandma in the whole entire universe. Please make her better. Amen.* I put the kneeler back up and sat back in the pew.

"Got the hang of it?" Grandpa asked.

"Yup! Got it!" I smiled, feeling as though I had just won a gold medal.

We walked back up to Grandma's room so we could kiss her goodbye. I held her hand as tears flooded from my eyes. *Don't you worry, Grandma. I'm praying. You're going to be just fine.* As I kissed her cheek goodbye, my face felt like fire, but my body was cold as ice just like Grandma's. Something didn't feel right. I felt like someone was watching me, but when I turned around, there was nobody there.

Donna M. Shogren, 61, of New Auburn went to be with her Lord Jesus on Wednesday, Aug. 29, 2007, at St. Mary's Hospital in Rochester, Minn.

Donna was born on June 8, 1946, in Bloomer to Arnold and Theresa (Schwartz) Motzer. She married Charles Shogren on Oct. 6, 1989, in New Auburn.

She was a member of St. Paul's Catholic Church and worked for Homeshield in Rice Lake for 18 years.

She is survived by: her husband, Charles of New Auburn; daughter, Shannon (Thomas) Berg of New Auburn; brothers, Tom (Annette) of Bloomer, Verlyn (Kathy) of New Auburn, Byron (Linda) of Chetek and Wayne (Alice) Motzer of New Auburn; two grandchildren, McKinze and Morgan Berg; she is also survived by several nieces and nephews.

She is preceded in death by: her parents; and one brother, Loren Motzer.

> Funeral services will be 11 a.m. Monday, Sept. 3 at St. Jude's Catholic Church, New Auburn, with Father James Arthur officiating. Burial will be at St. Paul's South Catholic Cemetery, Bloomer.

Life has never been the same since August 29, 2007. Even more so, life has never been the same since September 3, 2007. How could anything ever be the same after watching a machine lower a closed casket into a six-foot-deep hole, not to mention then having to watch dirt get thrown on top? Mom and Grandpa didn't actually let me stay for that part. They refused, but it didn't take a genius to know how the process worked. I was sent home with some family friends, but I didn't need to physically be there to watch it happen.

Every day and every night for years after the funeral, that's all I could see. In fact, to this day, when I return to the cemetery for a quick "hello," that's all I can see. For years, I blamed myself and felt that my family blamed me for her passing. They never said the words to my face, but it didn't matter. No matter what they did or didn't say, I couldn't forgive myself for the nasty words I had said to that woman. I knew it had to be God's way of punishing me for such cruel behavior.

God, why did you punish Grandma? She didn't do anything wrong. It was all my fault! Why didn't you take me instead? This was the question I asked for years but never could find the answer. I was struggling inside but couldn't ask for help; nobody ever wanted to talk about it. It was almost as if Grandma had never existed. All pictures were removed from the house, we never spoke her name, and we never talked about memories from the past. It was as if we got up the day after the funeral and said, "Oh well, life goes on."

That was far from the case, looking back on the situation as an adult. But as a grieving child, that's how I felt. It was like walking around day after day with a knife in the chest, and each day it got turned a little more.

I started the fourth grade the day after her funeral.

"Have a great day, sweetie. I'll see you after school!" Mom shouted as I slammed the car door.

Seriously? Have a great day? You just lost your mom, and I just lost my best friend, and I'm just supposed to act like nothing happened? Little did I know then that was going to be my reality for the next fifteen years. I got out of school that day and ran to the car. I was so excited about my day and all that I had learned, and then I began to cry the moment I sat in the front seat.

"Honey, what's wrong? Did something happen?" I didn't even want to ride in the car for the quarter mile we had to drive to get home. I would have done anything to just run away right then and never return.

"I just want Grandma!" I screamed at the top of my lungs as I began to wail.

"I know you do, sweetie. We all do," she said as she exited the school parking lot. "We're going to be alright; it's just going to take some time."

As ashamed as I am to admit this, I could have punched my mother right at that moment. At that point, I didn't think life could get any worse.

Growing up, I was fortunate enough to have my grandparents right across the street. Their house was a place I called home more than I did my own home. As far as I was concerned, my home was just a place where I slept and nothing more.

A few weeks later, I woke up before everyone else in my household. I came out to the living room, turned on the television, got my bowl of cereal, and sat on the couch. As I looked up to change the channel, I noticed something across the street out of the corner of my eye: FOR SALE BY OWNER. I ran to the window to make sure I was actually seeing what I was seeing. It was in bright orange letters on a black-and-white sign nailed to the tree: FOR SALE BY OWNER.

To this day, I can still see my child self, standing in the window, screaming and crying at the top of my lungs.

I ran across the street and up the stairs to find Grandpa coming out of the bathroom with nothing more than a towel around his waist. I didn't even care that I was looking at Grandpa half naked at this point, I just needed to know the answer. "What did I DO?! I can DO better. I can BE better!"

He went into the bedroom and shut the door to put some clothes on, and I started hitting the door. He swung open the door so fast it almost put a hole in the wall behind it, and he looked mad. "McKinze Olivia! Stop it! Stop it! You don't understand! It's just too hard!"

I had never heard my grandpa yell, let alone at me. He walked past me as if I didn't even exist and sat down in his "Boppa" chair—no explanation, no eye contact, no hug. Nothing. I had just lost my grandma, and now I was losing my grandpa too.

I was going to lose the man who taught me everything I know: how to ride a bike, how to cook, how to bake, how to be a decent member of society—and above all, how to love. Except on that day, it was as if I lost the ability to love—or that I never knew that it existed in the first place.

How could this man tell me that he loved me for a decade, every day and night, and then turn around and do this? That's not love, I thought in my head as I watched him pretend I wasn't standing there. In a matter of minutes, my heart went from mushy, gushy, and beating strong—a heart that loved everything and anyone—to nothing but a dark, cold, and hollow organ that was taking up space in my chest.

A few weeks later, I watched "Boppa" pull out of the driveway for the last time. He wasn't just moving down the road; he was moving to a completely different state eighteen hours away.

The only thing that remained that day was an empty house filled with memories, and for the last sixteen years, I've had to wake up and stare at that house and remind myself it's all that's left—memories. From the moment that FOR SALE sign was posted, I promised myself that I was never going to let another human being love me, nor was I going to actually ever love another human being ever again.

When you allow someone to love you or allow yourself to love someone else, you open yourself up for the possibility of getting hurt. *Block people out, and you won't get hurt. Don't have high expectations, or you will get hurt. They don't actually love you; you're not capable of being loved. Not even God loves you!* For years, those were the words engraved in my brain. Whenever my family, or anybody for that matter, would say, "I love you," I'd have to swallow hard, pretending I meant it when I said back, "I love you."

They don't love you. That's just what everybody says. Do you know how many times I've said, "I love you," in my life and not actually meant it? After 2007, up until about May of 2023, almost every single time.

Do you know how hard it is to *want* to love somebody so badly, but every part of your body is telling you, *Don't do it. They'll leave just like everyone else.* Do you know how hard it is to say, "I love you," and *want* to mean it, but you can't find it in your heart to do so?

Sure, I would throw out an "I love you" to every Tom, Dick, and Harry as they passed by, but did I mean it? Absolutely not! For so long, it was just another word in my vocabulary that had absolutely no meaning, much like my life as a whole at that time.

When Grandpa first left, we kept in touch, but it wasn't the same. I couldn't just call anytime I wanted anymore. I couldn't go over to the house anytime I wanted. Grandpa had moved on, and we were nothing but a memory. He moved away, got remarried, had new stepchildren and grandchildren that brought him joy. With each month that passed by, the contact with him became less and less. Eventually, there were no more phone calls, no more texts, no more letters, no more birthday cards, no more of anything. I had officially lost him too. There was no doubt about it.

We got the phone call on the morning of April 16, 2021. My dad turned fifty-six that day. We had the usual chocolate, chocolate cake, and candles all ready to go. Little did we know that there wasn't going to be much of a celebration that day. I was lying in bed that morning when Mom came in on the phone crying, "Grandpa Chuck passed away this morning."

I buried my head into my lap, but I didn't feel one bit of emotion. Of course, I cried, but the tears didn't feel real, nor did the emotions that came along with them. Let's face it; I had already lost him fourteen years prior. The only thing that I was really being told that morning was that his body was no longer here on this earth.

I went to work that night as if nothing happened, and even throughout the shift, I didn't feel one bit of emotion. I didn't think about him. I wasn't sad. I wasn't mad. I wasn't anything. On the way home that next morning, I wasn't paying attention. While on emotional autopilot, I hit a squirrel.

My heart had started to feel heavy. I was sleep-deprived, but now having to label myself as a squirrel murderer sent me completely over the edge. I pulled over to the side of the road, put it in park, and screamed at the top of my lungs as I punched the steering wheel. I cranked up the radio, put it to 106.7, and lo and behold, Grandpa's favorite song was just starting: "Rose Colored Glasses" by John Conlee. I know the song by heart but never actually took the time to truly listen to the lyrics.

How many of us look through the proverbial rose-colored glasses because we hate the thought of having to face the truth? The truth was that Grandpa was hurting, but he loved me with every ounce of his being. The truth was that I was hurting too, but I loved him with every ounce of mine—despite what happened. I thought that by looking at the world through rose-colored glasses, I would never get hurt.

But that wasn't reality and still isn't reality! The reality is that life is going to hurt, and it's going to absolutely suck at times! There are going to be times when you think it couldn't possibly get any worse, or it couldn't possibly get any better. What is it going to take for you to lay aside those rose-colored glasses?

Do you know not only how long but also *what* it took for me to remove the glasses? Everything. Absolutely everything. It took accepting people into my life again, knowing that I'd get hurt. It took allowing people into my heart, accepting I'd get hurt. It took my pride. Took humbling myself to others. It took a therapist, a new church, fasting, tithing, and, above all, it took a whole lot of Jesus. It took being able to get up one morning and looking myself dead in the eyes in the bathroom mirror, saying, *Kinze! You have to stop! It doesn't have to be this way.*

Chapter 8

COME ON IN; THE WATER'S FINE

When you pass through the waters, I will be with you; and when you pass through the rivers, they will not sweep over you. When you walk through the fire, you will not be burned; the flames will not set you ablaze.

Isaiah 43:2

I started attending the open houses at Chippewa Valley Technical College (CVTC) my freshman year of high school. From freshman to senior year, I attended every fall and spring open house—and every community event in between. I had passed the college multiple times throughout my lifetime, but never in a million years did I think I'd actually be going there after graduating from high school.

You see, with my extensive medical history, primarily involving my gastrointestinal tract, it was my ultimate dream to be a pediatric surgeon specializing in gastroenterology so that I could work alongside the surgeons at Children's Minnesota, the children's hospital in St. Paul, Minnesota, who helped save my life, time and time again.

As I began to seriously think about my future and the reality of things, I came to the realization that medical school was too far out of my reach. It wasn't an impossible thought, just something that wasn't within my reach at the time. I know what you may be thinking: "No dream is ever too big or too small if your heart's in it."

But that was the thing; my heart really wasn't in it. I had lived a life in hospitals, with treatment, and surgeries, and imaging, tubes, and, and, and. It was constant. I missed out on my childhood, grew up way faster than any child should, my family had to make extreme sacrifices, and my sister's education and emotional needs were neglected because everyone was always focused on me and whether I was going to live or die that day.

So why would I want to personally live that life and then turn around and go to work there too? The more I thought about it, the more I was drawn away from the idea, and the thought of Dr. McKinze Berg just didn't have a nice ring to it anymore. It wasn't that I didn't want to help children like me. Nor that I didn't want to do the research and find the answers. It was a selfish act that I couldn't make it both my personal and professional life; it would have been too much. It would have eaten me alive, and I'm not ashamed to admit that. Everyone has limits, and that would have been mine.

I had my first-ever tour of the college in the fall of my freshman year. We toured all programs on both the business education and healthcare side. I had explored the list of degree options prior to coming, but nothing really grabbed my attention. I don't know if you've ever attended a college open house, but in my opinion, it's *lame*! You get put with a group of strangers, nobody seems to have any interest in being there, the instructors are trying hard to sell their programs to you, nobody's taking the bait, and everyone looks as if they're just there for community service hours. When I first attended, I felt so out of place, and I was very uncomfortable.

"So, to the right here, we have our Respiratory Therapy program. Would anybody be interested in taking a look at this program?" Shelly Olson was the dean at the time of giving the tour, and my mom and I loved her the moment she said hello.

It was rare to see someone take pride in their job and actually enjoy it. With Shelly, it was obvious that her calling was exactly this—not giving tours but being "Mother Hen" of CVTC. Mom and I wanted to check out the program, but nobody had raised their hand, so we decided to stop back in on our way out. We went down the hall a little farther and explored some other programs, but nobody seemed interested.

"I don't want to do the group tour anymore. Can we leave?" I asked Mom, my disappointment undisguised.

"Sure, but can we stop back and check out the Respiratory Therapy program before we leave?" she asked with that usual smirk and eyebrow raise.

We walked into the classroom, and my chest felt like it was on fire. He had such a familiar face. *He looks exactly like grandpa.*

"Come on in; the water's fine!" he said, extending a hand. "Don Raymond, program director. And this is Theresa Meinen. She's also an instructor and is our clinical director."

I shook his hand, and that's all I needed. I decided at that exact moment that my calling wasn't to be a doctor but a respiratory therapist. They said that I was only a freshman and that I still had a way to go before being eligible to consider coming to the college. But they gave me every sheet of information and every detail possible about the program and career. We left that evening and came back for an open house that following spring. The following fall, we were there again, and the spring after that. I hadn't even applied for the program yet, and I had already claimed Don and Theresa as my second set of parents. It was official; they were stuck with me.

In the fall of my senior year of high school, I sent off the application to CVTC for the Respiratory Therapy program, and in early spring, there was a letter in the mail addressed to McKinze Berg from Chippewa Valley Technical College. I tore open the letter and began to read as my family stood around eating their fingers like popcorn. "Dear McKinze Berg, Congratulations! We are incredibly pleased to announce that you have been accepted into the Respiratory Therapy program starting in the Fall of 2016." Of course, there was other information on that page, but when I saw the word "Congratulations," that's all I needed.

On May 18, 2018, I stood on the ramp in the auditorium as I anxiously waited to hear my name called to walk across the stage to receive my diploma.

"This is it! Congratulations, kiddo. I'm so proud of you!" Shelly said as she hugged me tight with tears in her eyes.

On June 30, 2018, I turned twenty years old. How many twenty-year-olds drive to Woodbury, Minnesota, on their birthday to sit in front of a computer and take a test that determines their entire future? Not many. That day, I received the best birthday gift ever: the piece of paper that deemed me an official respiratory therapist.

That July, I started my career and was over the moon to finally be considered "one of them." I flew through orientation, and before I knew it, I was on my own. Looking back on the moment, it's a really crazy thought! Most twenty-year-olds can barely take care of themselves, and I was left in charge of people's lives and machines and treatments that literally keep them alive.

I celebrated my five-year anniversary in 2023, and still, to this day, I can't believe it. A lot has happened in five years—a lot of lives saved and changed, including my own.

When I was in college, I was a mentor who helped individuals inside and outside of the program. At times, it was frustrating, but

I was blessed to be an individual to which academics always came easy. I always worked hard and studied hard because I had severe anxiety if I didn't. But at the end of the day, I always did very well. I felt so bad for people that struggled; my heart really went out to them. Everybody is here for the same reason: to get an education and do something purposeful with their lives.

I was approached one day by someone who happened to be a year behind me in the program. She was struggling severely, and if she didn't pass this one exam, there were no more chances for her. She was going to be done and would have to leave the program. For weeks, we met at different locations and went over the material hundreds of times. I'd usually show up at the coffee shop or college before her, and every time she came in, she looked as if she needed something to throw up into.

"Come on in; the water's fine!" I said as she sat down with her belongings.

"You hang out with Don too much." She gave the same response every time.

This girl knew exactly what she was doing and talking about. Her problem wasn't that she didn't know the material. Her problem was that every time she sat down to take an exam, her brain was left at home. She had so much test anxiety that she could barely function before and after the exam, and when she'd get her results, it was even worse. She needed help, but it was more than I could offer. Even though it wasn't *my* help she needed, I continued to show up whenever she asked and helped her in any way that I was able.

I got a text on the night of Sunday, March 18: "Hey girl! Sorry this is really last minute, but can you come over to my house tomorrow? I have an exam on Tuesday, and I'm really freaking out! HELP!"

I looked at my calendar and replied, "No worries! See you at 1:00?"

I packed up my notes and books that afternoon and headed down. The roads weren't terrible, despite it being the day after one of the biggest ice storms Wisconsin had ever seen. However, every now and then, I'd hit a patch of ice, and my wheels would spin.

I got to her house and walked in to find her pacing her living room. I looked around, and there were whiteboards, books, papers, trifold boards, and empty energy drink cans spread all over the room as if she were trying to win this year's Nobel Peace Prize.

"OK! I think I got it! Hear me out, and make sure I'm getting this right. I have to pass this test!" she said as I could see her hands trembling from the caffeine and anxiety that had taken over her body.

I stared at her for a moment, concerned, and said, "Honey, why don't we just take a little break. Have you eaten today? Maybe I could go grab us lunch." I started searching her cupboards and fridge, both of which were almost bare.

"NO! I have to pass this test!" She cut me off immediately. She stepped back to look at the whiteboard as she chewed off every last one of her fingernails.

I sat her down on the couch and began my pep talk. "You know exactly what you're doing; that isn't the problem. When you sit down for the exam tomorrow, I want you to do one question at a time. Cover up the answers; answer the question first in your head. After you answer the question, look at the answers. If the answer you said in your head is on there, circle it and move on. DO NOT re-read the question. Move on. When you're done, make sure that you answered every question and turn it in. Don't re-read or change answers; just hand it in. You know what you're doing!" Nothing I was saying was getting to her.

She got up and continued pacing the living room. Her breathing became heavy, and I could see her pulse coming out of her neck.

What do you do when someone is having a panic attack? If it's situational, you remove them from the situation or environment that is triggering them, right?

"Let's take the dog for a walk. She looks like she has to go to the bathroom," I offered.

I grabbed the leash, attached it to her collar, and we went out the door. As we rounded the corner, her breathing began to slow, her pulse slowly settling back into her neck. *Alright, now we're getting somewhere.*

"KINZE! Kinze, are you OK? Hold on. I'm calling 9-1-1."

She was white as a sheet.

What happened?

I looked up at her six heads. "What? No, why?" I was flat on my back, and I was freezing. *Why does my head hurt? What in the world? Is that blood?*

"Kinze, don't move, you slipped and you hit your head really hard. Please, don't move, I'm calling an ambulance. You were out for quite a while." She struggled to take her phone out of her pocket as she tried to keep the dog from running away. Her face was whiter than the snow, her hands trembling.

"Here, give me the phone." I reached for it but couldn't tell which one it was of the multiples in my vision. "I don't need a dang ambulance. Just help me up, will ya? I'm fine!" I put the phone in my pocket.

I sat up for a little bit and let my eyes straighten out in my head before standing up. "Kinze, you need to go get checked out. You're bleeding." She tried to grab my coat.

"Ya got an ice pack? Then we're good. Are you coming?" I started walking back toward the house.

We got back to the house, and I wiped the blood from the back of my head. She got an ice pack from the freezer, and there was a knock at the door. It was another girl from the program, and with her was a beautiful yellow lab with a black and red vest labeled SERVICE DOG.

It wasn't always this way, but I'm allergic to most animals, especially those with long hair. For some reason, the ones I'm most allergic to love to come as close to me as possible. How ironic. I sat on the couch with the ice pack on the back of my head, and this dog would not leave me alone. Every two seconds, he'd nudge my leg, and before I knew it, his paws were on my lap. I love animals, but today, I was not in the mood.

"Wow, he doesn't usually take to strangers very well. That's really interesting, you must be some sort of dog whisperer." His owner chuckled as she tried to remove him from my lap. The minute his owner tried to pull him down, he was right back up.

I tried pushing him away, but now his entire body was on my lap, and he was licking my face. As I began to speak, I could feel the color drain from my face. I tried to speak, but I couldn't come up with the right words to say, and any words I did say were slurred as if I had just spent the entire day at the bar.

"Whoa! Are you OK?!" His owner asked, with a puzzled look on her face.

No, I'm not OK.

"No, she's not OK! This idiot just slipped and fell, went unconscious, her head is bleeding, and she's refusing to go in!" My mentee continued to yell at the poor girl as if this was her fault.

Geez. Nothing like throwing someone under the bus.

"That's it. I'm calling an ambulance! Where's my phone? You're going in." She tried digging in my pockets, but I handed her the phone before she had the chance.

"Fine. But I'm not going by ambulance. You're driving." I took a deep breath and stood up ever so slowly.

We got to the Emergency Department entrance, and the moment I opened the car door, I threw up. My head felt like it was in a vice, I couldn't see straight, and I couldn't stand up without tipping over. The registration girl came out with a wheelchair, but I could barely find it to sit down. I got inside and back to a room, and all the drama started. Thankfully, my mentee was able to answer some of the questions, but she was able to find my cell phone to dial my mom to get there as soon as possible. I stared at the ceiling, trying to keep my eyes open.

"We don't know. They're taking her down for a scan to see if she has a brain bleed. She fell and hit her head and split it open pretty good, but they don't think she'll need staples. She's awake. Everything looks OK physically. They said she definitely has a concussion. She can't really talk right now because her speech is a little messed up. Just get here." *Click*" She slammed the phone on the bedside table.

I went down for the scan, and all I could think was, *This is stupid. Just let me go home and sleep it off. I'll be fine by morning. I got things to do. I got a job to go to. Just give me some Tylenol and send me home.*

When I got back to the room, the girls had already left, but there was a knock on the door not long after.

"Well, kiddo, I got good news and bad news. Good news is we don't have to operate on your brain. Bad news is there's some swelling and a questionable small bleed. It's not big enough to operate on, but you're going to have to stay a night or two just so we can make sure it doesn't get worse."

At this point, I was just shocked that they actually saw a brain on the scan. It may not work all the time, but at least there is a scan available for proof.

I took a second to respond and stuttered (the result of the brain injury that unfortunately stuck for some time. Embarrassing, but I got over it.) "And if I decide to go home?"

The physician assistant looked at me as though I had made the most unreasonable request. "I beg your pardon?"

"And if I decide to go home? I'm not staying here. My only complaint is a headache, and I'm sure with some rest everything else will fall into place. I know the drill; I work here. I may be stubborn, but I'm not stupid. It's not like I'm going to go home and go skydiving. Bed rest until I follow up with someone. And schedule another scan." I held out my pinky as if that were going to be the one thing that convinced her to let me go.

I could see the wheels turning in her head. *Ooooooooooh, she brought out the pinky promise. This girl means business!* She probably could have begged to differ and probably thought, *The only therapy you need is a padded room upstairs—and maybe some restraints so you'll actually rest.*

Mom came in through the door just as the nurse was coming in with my discharge paperwork.

"Come on in; the water's fine," I stuttered as she stared at me in amazement that I was still alive and in one piece. "They said I can go home. I just have to follow up with neurology and start some therapies to fix the rest. Bed rest until then, and if anything gets worse, I just come back."

Mom stared at me for a few seconds. "Your speech is like this, and they're sending you home? Are you freaking kidding me?"

Needless to say, she was absolutely livid. I swallowed and stuck to the script I had pre-planned in my head. "Yeah, they said it's pretty common with all brain injuries. It's like shaking a bottle of pop and taking off the cap. It stops exploding eventually. The scans didn't show anything major, so we're going to just redo a scan before I see neurology and make sure I'm on the right track."

It was a quiet ride home, but once I was in my own bed, I was already starting to feel a little better. The next morning, I woke up and felt as if I had just gotten hit by a truck. *What in the world happened yesterday?* I got out of bed and immediately had to sit back down because the room was spinning so bad. I tried to stand up again, but my body just wasn't having it. *Was I drugged? Nope. Just stupid. You probably should have stayed.* I crawled out of my bedroom to the couch. I don't know how I got to my appointment that day, but somehow, we managed to get me into the car, and off we went.

I sat in the waiting room and waited for my name to be called.

"Want me to come back with you or stay here," Mom asked.

"Oh no, that's OK. I can go back myself." I stood up and started to stumble toward the medical assistant who called my name.

While I sat in the exam room, my knee started to bounce, and my hands began to sweat. A few minutes later, the nurse practitioner entered the room and sat down. "Alright, Kinze. One question right off the bat just to get it out of the way. Are you always this stupid, or is this new since the accident?" she asked with a grin.

"It's genetic." I sarcastically replied.

The appointment didn't last very long, but I definitely had a long road ahead. I went from being a fully functioning respiratory therapist and saving lives every day to now, once again, being the patient who had to do her own healing.

After over a year of physical therapy, occupational therapy, and a whole lot more of speech therapy, I was basically as good as new. I was able to go back to work. I was having the time of my life doing what I love, until—

Lights out.

I woke up to a room full of coworkers staring at me. *Now, what happened?!* I was absolutely furious at this point.

"Your heart rate is out of control, and your blood pressure spikes then drops the moment you move. Do you have a heart condition we need to know about? Maybe you came back to work too soon. You're going through a lot right now. Your body is still processing things. Maybe it was too soon?" The nurse and provider shared a concerned look.

I took the blood pressure cuff and pulse oximeter off and threw it on the bed. I stormed out of the room and back to my office. I was drenched in sweat but was cold and clammy.

One of the nurses followed me into the office. "Kinze. What the heck is going on? Are you sure you're OK?"

I wiped the sweat from my eyes. "Yeah, I think I just got overheated. I'm fine."

I went to stand up, then fell back into the chair.

"Kinze, you are not OK. You need to go get checked out." She tried to grab my arm, but I pulled it away.

"Really, I'm fine. I didn't sleep enough yesterday, and I definitely haven't had enough water this shift. Let me chug this bottle, eat a little salt, and I'll be fine. Promise." I escaped into the bathroom, hoping she would leave me alone.

The following morning, I was pulled into the office by my boss and a representative from Human Resources. "Kinze, we don't think you're ready to come back to work. We're taking you off the schedule until you go and see somebody to figure out what is going on. You're not getting fired. We just want to make sure you're OK. We don't want something happening to you while you're caring for patients. We need you to sign these documents, and then we're done here."

I ripped the pen so fast out of the poor girl's hand and signed the paper so hard I think I put a hole in it. I stormed out of the office, bawling my eyes out.

I just want to be a normal, FREAKING PERSON! Why do things keep happening?

As you can imagine, there were definitely more than a few choice words thrown in there, as well. I sped home, got into the house, and spiraled out of control. "You pass out once, maybe a few times, and you're out!"

Mom stood up from the kitchen table, pulling me in for a hug. "Kinze, just calm down. It's going to get figured out. You'll get checked out, pass all of their tests, and you'll be back to work in no time at all. It's going to be OK. Just take a breath."

As the days and weeks went on, I was getting worse. I went from passing out a couple times here and there to once a day, then to twenty times a day. My labs looked great, other than a few electrolyte imbalances. My imaging was fine, and the doctors said, "We don't know. We want to send you to a neurologist in Rochester, but you're going to need to do some tests prior." I jumped through all the hoops, completed all the tests, and found myself sitting on the Neurology floor waiting to be called back.

"You have a condition called POTS (Postural Orthostatic Tachycardia Syndrome) with orthostatic hypotension (blood pressure drops with standing). It's totally fixable. You just need to drink more water, add more salt into your diet, wear compression stockings and a compression band around your waist, and start an exercise program that focuses on lower body strengthening." I shook her hand, grabbed my "Return to Work" note, and went about life.

I was doing everything I was told at that time. I didn't feel great, but I noticed little improvements here and there. A couple weeks went by, and I just felt like I was getting weaker by the day. I got up one afternoon, put on my scrubs, and headed to work.

"Kinze. Your blood pressure is so high, I'm surprised that you're not actively having a stroke." I woke up in the Emergency Department, mad as a hornet. I tore the blood pressure cuff and pulse oximeter off and threw it on the bed. I ripped the gown off and put my clothes back on.

"I'm fine," I said as I stormed out of the department.

The next day, I was back in the "interrogation room" with two familiar faces. I think you can figure out for yourself how the conversation went.

A few weeks later, I was back in a very familiar environment.

"I'm going to put in a referral for physical therapy," the Rochester neurologist said as she typed vigorously on her keyboard.

I got nauseated at the idea of having to return to physical therapy. I was going for weeks with minimal improvement noted.

One day as I was on the stationary bike, my therapist began to tell me about some research she had been doing.

"Let's face it, Kinz, I don't specialize in this, but I think I can find someone who can. I was talking to a coworker the other day, and as soon as I said 'POTS,' she said, 'OH! My best friend has that! She had to go to Texas to get treatment, but she's doing really well. Let me text her and make sure it's OK that I give you her number.'"

My therapist gave me the number, and I texted her as soon as I got home. "Hi there, my name is Kinze, and I received your number from my physical therapist. I was just reaching out to hear about your experience with POTS-care."

It took a couple of days, but I finally got a response back. I read her story—how well she's doing now. But one thing stood out: "It sucks, but they don't take insurance. But if you have $8,600, I promise that it's worth it!"

I automatically started laughing. *Oh yeah, let me just pull that money right out of my rainy day fund. Are you CRAZY? $8,600? It's no wonder sick people give up. Who can afford it?*

I didn't respond to the message for a while. Instead, I paced back and forth in the kitchen, wondering which organ I could sell to get the $8,600. It was crazy expensive, but I needed to do something, or I was going to jump off the roof. Heck, I wouldn't even have to jump. Just put the wheelchair near the edge, let me stand, and the rest would take care of itself. My parents came home, and I began to cry.

My dad came upstairs with a worried look on his face. "Are you OK?"

I couldn't answer.

"Do you need help?" His jaw hung open.

I nodded my head yes and buried my face in his chest. "There's this program in Texas that could potentially save my life, but it's $8,600. They don't take insurance—"

He cut me off. "Then we're going to Texas. We'll get the money, I promise. We'll do whatever it takes."

I've never asked for a penny in my life, but I knew I had to put my pride aside.

Later that evening, my grandma (Dad's mom) called. I still hadn't recovered but answered the phone anyway.

"Hi, Grandma," I said as I wiped the snot and tears with my sleeve.

"Kinze. Oh my gosh, honey. What's the matter?" My grandma and I never really had a close relationship, at least not like the relationship I had with my maternal grandmother. I never filled her in on anything. Everything was always fine. I was always fine; I was always a broken record when I talked to her. I only saw her on holidays and talked to her maybe once a month.

I knew that if I said, "Nothing," I wasn't going to get very far. I wasn't even convincing myself at this point. "Grandma, I'm sick. And there's this program in Texas, but it's $8,600, and I'm just really scared and need to do something."

I heard a laugh on the other end. "Well, Kinzer, I'll take care of it, sweetie."

I started bawling. I hardly had a relationship with this woman, and there was absolutely no way I was going to take her money. "Grandma, I could never ask you to do that."

"Kinzer, you didn't ask. I offered. I'm your grandma for crying out loud. Let me help!" she said.

I paused on the other end before answering, sobbing into my already snotted-up sweatshirt sleeve. *You did too ask. You asked the moment you started crying to her about it. You ain't fooling nobody. You may not have asked her directly for the money, but you asked. You should have never opened that can of worms. Now you have to live with that.*

Two weeks later, I was on a Zoom call, and about six months later, I was back to work for good. I no longer had to do therapies, but I had to consume thirty-eight pills per day, come into the clinic for weekly lab draws, and wear so many harnesses I could barely breathe. But at least I felt somewhat human and could return back to a "normal" life.

On my first overnight back at work, I was sitting in the office chair when I heard footsteps come into the office in the morning. It was my boss.

I quickly spun around in the chair with a greeting known to many. "Well, good morning, sunshine! Come on in; the water's fine!"

Chapter 9

EVICTION NOTICE

Submit yourselves, then, to God. Resist the devil, and he will flee from you.

James 4:7

He never signed a lease. He just kind of moved in one day and took over. I already had a tenant and wasn't looking for another one. But he just showed up looking for a place to stay. He was severely sunburned, the soles of his shoes were worn out, and he looked like he hadn't slept or eaten in days.

I had heard of him but never thought I'd ever meet him face-to-face. I had heard about what he had done, the pain he caused, and everything he stole from people, but I couldn't help but feel sorry for him. He talked really smoothly, had a gentle smile, pretty eyes, and swore up and down that he had changed. It was as if he was trying to sell me a Lamborghini Veneno, and instead of taking it for a test drive, I just bought it.

One day, Tenant #1 and I were in the kitchen while Tenant #2 lay on the couch, eating pizza, playing video games.

Tenant #1 paced the kitchen angrily but remained calm. "I go to work every day, I pay my rent on time, I'm clean, and I've never asked you for anything! He's jobless, doesn't pay rent, treats you like trash, and doesn't do anything but make our lives miserable. Either you kick him out, or I'm leaving."

I stared at him in disbelief. *How could he make me choose? This man was just hitting a rough patch in his life. I wasn't going to kick him while he was down.*

"I guess that settles it then. I'll be out by morning," Tenant #1 said as he backed slowly out of the kitchen.

I felt really bad, but he had his life figured out. Tenant #2, on the other hand, just needed some time to figure out his.

After a few months, I knew exactly what was happening. I was being used, but every time I tried to address the situation, I couldn't. I was getting uncomfortable, but I felt frozen. I had given him plenty of time to find a job and another place to stay, but it always seemed as though there was an excuse. He went from taking up residence to taking up parties. Every. Single. Night.

What was once a comforting home was now a dark space filled with empty beer cans, vodka bottles, and lost hope.

I got home from work one night, and I could hear the stereo blaring before I even opened my car door. I walked through the door to a house filled with strangers and the smell of weed.

"Hey, everybody! This is Kinze!" He did everything he could to bring attention to my existence.

I stood in the foyer with my jaw at my ankles. Next thing I knew, they were all hanging on me, chanting my name, and I was taking shots faster than they could hand them to me. The next night was the same, and the night after that, and the night after that. Before I knew it, I was "one of them."

Every morning, I'd continue to get up and go to work, but all I could think about was the fun I would have when I got home. As

I'd drive home, I'd chant to myself: *KINZE! KINZE! KINZE! And the crowd. Goes. Wild!*

It was the same routine several nights of the week, and after a while, I began to feel it. It started weighing on not only my physical health but my mental health. I tried to quit, but it was too late. It had become a problem. Day by day, I got sucked down a little further, and a little further, until one day, it was almost too far.

On the Saturday after my twenty-fifth birthday, I woke up to beautiful weather, and I was going to accomplish one of my biggest fears: floating the river. I know it's not very exciting, but you wouldn't believe the amount of "normal people" things I haven't done in my lifetime. Believe it or not, one of the best things about gaining friends is being able to accomplish a lot of firsts with them. I'm thankful for the people in my life. They've taught me what it's like to *live*!

I looked in the bathroom mirror as I got dressed for the day and gave myself a pep talk. *Alright. Don't be stupid today. You can have a few, but you're not on land today. Take your four-pack and enough water to flush it out. You can do it! Go get 'em tiger!*

I got in the car, and I was on my way.

I pulled into the driveway and sat there for a few minutes before working up the courage to go inside. We had a great breakfast, got in the car, and headed for the river. I was a little nervous, but once I was in, I was in!

Why have I not done this before? This is so relaxing!

We floated a little way before I cracked open the first drink.

Slow and steady. Slow and steady.

I finished the first drink and realized that I'd forgotten my water bottle in the car. I waited a little while longer, and I cracked open the second.

You're doing good. Slow and steady.

I sipped slowly as I listened to the playlist blast across the wide-open river. I wasn't really partaking in any of the conversations around me. I was just soaking it all in. Of course, I'd throw a comment or a laugh in here and there, but I wasn't paying much attention. I don't always like conversation. Sometimes, I just enjoy people's presence.

I should have said no. If someone ever offers you a Bahama Mama in a can after you've already had a few too many, and your goal is to remember the moment, just say no. Don't ask me what happened. I don't remember. I looked through my phone the following day at a couple pictures that were taken on the river. I zoomed in, and in my hand was the dreaded drink.

That. That is the last thing I remember.

I don't know how they got me into the house. I don't know how they got me out of the water. My face hurt, I had a bruise on my arm, and my back looked as though I'd taken a beating.

"Dude, you almost died. No joke, we had to throw you back into the tube, and you tried to jump out so many times. And then the one time you jumped out, you passed out and had a seizure, and we had to try to keep your head above water and not lose the tubes at the same time." My friend sat on the opposite side of the couch with a concerned look on her face.

I had just crawled off the couch in clothes I hadn't shown up in. I was sick to my stomach—not only from the amount of alcohol I just pounded but from what I was hearing.

I got up off the couch, stumbled to the bathroom, and changed back into my original clothes. "What do I have to do to prove to you I can drive home?" I asked.

"Well, you're not speaking gibberish anymore, your eyes are focused, and you're walking straight," she said as she pulled the keys off the top of the fridge and handed them to me. "Let me know when you get home, and if you get down the road and need a ride, call me."

I was so disgusted with myself. How could I let it get this bad? I apologized more times than I could even count.

"Kinze. It was your birthday. It's not like you're doing this all the time." She tried so hard to comfort me, but she didn't know that this had become an "all the time" thing. Nobody did; not even my own family.

I woke up the next morning in a panic. I was lying on my right side, and it was as if the voice had whispered through my pillow into my ear, *Do you know what's happening in your home?* If anybody were going to whisper anything, why would it be that?

I opened my Bible that morning and picked up where I had left off at Genesis 25:24–34.

> When the time came for her to give birth, there were twin boys in her womb. The first to come out was red, and his whole body was like a hairy garment; so they named him Esau. After this, his brother came out, with his hand grasping Esau's heel; so he was named Jacob. Isaac was sixty years old when Rebekah gave birth to them.
>
> The boys grew up, and Esau became a skillful hunter, a man of the open country, while Jacob was content to stay at home among the tents. Isaac, who had a taste for wild game, loved Esau, but Rebekah loved Jacob.
>
> Once when Jacob was cooking some stew, Esau came in from the open country, famished. He said to Jacob, "Quick, let me have some of that red stew! I'm famished!" (That is why he was also called Edom [Red].)
>
> Jacob replied, "First sell me your birthright."

"Look, I am about to die," Esau said. "What good is the birthright to me?"

But Jacob said, "Swear to me first." So he swore an oath to him, selling his birthright to Jacob.

Then Jacob gave Esau some bread and some lentil stew. He ate and drank, and then got up and left.

So Esau despised his birthright.

Perhaps you read that and said, "What's your point?"

My point is that this passage got me thinking about what it means to be a child of God—a child of God with an inheritance who would be willing to sell out everything for temporary gratification. I'm not interpreting the Scripture here, but it made me realize after reading it that I *did* care about my "rights" as the firstborn daughter, but not like I should have.

I cared about what people thought. I cared about if I was going to be judged for my beliefs. I cared about the fact that it was a possibility that I was going to be labeled as the "crazy Bible thumper." I knew what was happening in my own "home," but I refused to look it straight in the eye at the dinner table.

I don't care about what people think or say about me! What I care about is my relationship with him. What I care about is representing Christ and representing him well."

I sat at the kitchen table that morning, staring out the patio window. I broke down into tears and thought about how I would talk about this. Alcoholism runs in my family on both sides; some were saved, others not so much.

"You just need to learn to drink in moderation." That's what they all said.

If I had a penny for every time I'd heard that over the past however many months, I'd be rich. Moderation was not key anymore when it came to alcohol; the word was no longer even in my dictionary.

I have a problem. I didn't think I did, but I do. I don't want to be that friend that people have to stop having fun around because I'm a safety concern. I imagined myself having millions of conversations with my parents, but this wasn't one of them.

They knew how hard this was. My father had been sober for two decades, and my mom kept drinking to a minimum when she saw how much alcoholism affected her family. Growing up, we never really had alcohol in the house, specifically for that reason. It was never something I incorporated into my life, so when I did, it got out of control.

I started attending meetings online but never actually participated. I listened to testimonies on YouTube and reviewed The Twelve Steps. I bought every daily devotional book and journal I could find. I removed myself from those who loved to drink and party, and I prayed and read my Bible even more. I wasn't going to let this affect me like it affected my family. I absolutely refused. I didn't judge those around me who continued to partake in these activities, but I knew I had to distance myself because it was a problem for me.

I returned home from a difficult shift at work a couple of weeks later. We'd lost one patient, removed a machine keeping someone alive a few rooms down as they transitioned to hospice care, watched a young child grieve the loss of his father in the family lounge, and had a patient go downhill at the end of shift. That's the life of a healthcare worker. You never know what's going to happen.

Some people think that because we work in healthcare and see all sorts of tragedies that it's easy for us in those situations because at the end of the day we get to go home to our families. You're right, I am incredibly grateful to return home to my family after those shifts—and that it wasn't me that had to say goodbye. But that doesn't mean I don't experience basic human feelings in those moments.

What people don't see are the tears that we shed in our cars after we clock out. They don't see the hours of sleep we lose because whenever we close our eyes, we can still see that child's face or hear the wails of the family as the news is delivered that they didn't make it. They don't see the moment in the Walmart parking lot when someone comes up to you and says, "You probably don't remember me, but you removed my mom from the ventilator a few weeks ago. I just wanted to thank you for the care you gave her and for being with us in her final moments."

It never used to be this way, but eventually, I didn't deal with the emotions. I covered them up with a drink.

I came home that evening and did something I wasn't used to doing. I dealt with my emotions. I sat out on the deck with a glass of water, pulled out my Bible and a journal, and began to write. I wrote about ten pages before I finally put it aside. The sun was setting, the breeze was light, the birds were singing in the trees, and the guy in the trailer court was yelling for his hound, Ollie, for the billionth time in five minutes. I sat in silence and began to simply observe my surroundings.

It's amazing how much you can work through and recognize when there aren't beer goggles or rose-colored glasses to look through. I worked through the feelings, dealt with the emotions, and believe it or not, I got a full ten hours of sleep that night without interruption.

You're probably asking at this point, "Hey wait a minute, that's great and all, but what happened to the tenants?" and "What does any of this have to do with anything you have written in this chapter?"

Here's the thing. The only tenants that I ever had, and the ones you will ever have, are the ones living inside of you. But it's up to you to decide which one you're going to let live there and take up space.

For years, Tenant #1 (Jesus) remained loyal and faithful. He never failed me and always followed through for me, even in times that were life-threatening and life-altering. I may have kicked him out, but there was never a time that he wasn't standing in the distance, witnessing my every move. Why? Because he loves me!

He continued to break my fall until he let me see what would happen if I fell flat on my face. He loved me, but he loved me enough to let me experience the consequences of my choices. But even when I face-planted, who was the first to lend me a hand and wipe the tears? God that did that for me—and he can and will do that for you. If you let him.

Needless to say, Tenant #1 moved back in, and we are recreating our relationship. On the other hand, after the ongoing life struggles, the near drowning, and the acceptance of my drinking problem, I ended up drafting a letter to Tenant #2. The letter looked a little something like this:

EVICTION NOTICE

July 2, 2023

TENANT: Devil

RESIDENCE: Kinze Berg

This serves as notice that you have been evicted from the property effective **IMMEDIATELY.**

Your presence on this property without permission from the manager is a crime and will be dealt with for failure to comply. You will be held responsible for the damage that has been done during your time of stay, and you will be held accountable if damage is done to the property post-eviction.

Thank you for your cooperation,
McKinze Berg

Chapter 10

BRAND-SPANKIN' NEW

The nations will see your vindication, and all kings your glory; you will be called by a new name that the mouth of the LORD will bestow.

Isaiah 62:2

"You're going to be the death of me. You know that?" The door opened, and she dropped her head.

I patted Benchie before popping up. "Nice to see you too, Jen. Welcome to session eleven!"

That's how I started all my therapy sessions this time around: "Good morning/afternoon, welcome to session ___. How nice of you to join me." I don't know why she finds it so funny, but she laughs every time. I took a seat in my usual spot on the left side of the couch, closest to her chair.

"So now what happened?" she asked, scratching her head as if she knew a good story was about to flee from my mouth.

"Stupidity," I responded, sitting there in my neck brace, arm limply at my side.

She didn't seem amused and continued to stare at me with *that look* I tend to receive from her quite often.

"We're not really sure what's going on, I guess. I've still got MRIs and other appointments to attend. It's possible that something in my neck and shoulder detached from my spinal cord, or something is maybe compressed; we don't know. About two years ago, I fell off a ten-foot ladder while loading some boxes into the rafters. Coming down, I missed the second to last step from the top, and I came straight down onto my left shoulder. I popped it out of place, got it put back in, and went about my life.

"About a year later, I started to notice that I was getting weaker on my left side, and it was getting harder and harder to lift my arm. I did everything: physical therapy, massage therapy, chiropractic, acupuncture, prayer, etc. Then, about three months ago, I finally decided I should go get it checked out, and I got a cortisone shot that lasted for about a day. A couple Thursday's ago, I began to have stroke-like symptoms on my left side. My face began to droop, my speech was slurred, and my arm dropped dead at my side, turning purple and cold. Then, Friday—"

Her mouth hung wide open, eyes wide as saucers. "Oh my gosh. Hold on! What did the ER say?"

I chuckled and hung my head sheepishly. "Oh! I didn't go to the ER because I already had an appointment scheduled for that Friday with my primary."

She began to rub her face vigorously with her hands and almost pulled her hair out of her head in such frustration.

"So, Friday, I was eating breakfast, and as I went to take a bite, my head dropped forward as if it broke off my body." I shifted in the chair, ready for a lecture.

I could tell she wanted to get out of her chair and throat-punch me. "And then you went to the ER, right?"

I shared a suspicious smile. "No, I went to the appointment I already had scheduled."

I'll tell you, if looks could kill, I would have been dead right then and there.

"I thought it could wait!" I said as I shrugged the one shoulder I could lift.

The following Sunday, a friend picked me up for church. I went in and sat down in my usual spot, but something didn't feel right. It actually wasn't that something didn't feel right; it was that I didn't feel anything at all. Something in my heart told me to get up and move, so I stood up and walked over to the other side of the church and stood in the corner. As I closed my eyes and began to worship. I started to cry.

Despite my current situation with the neurological and gastro-intestinal struggles, I actually didn't feel anything weighing super heavily on my heart, but God was trying to tell me something different. I ended up sitting in the middle section that night while Pastor Char talked about identity. Identity is something that we talk about heavily in our church because it's the biggest thing we forget at times. We forget that our identity isn't what we do. It's who we are in the eyes of Jesus Christ, and we need to remember that we are a son/daughter of God.

I've cried in church (I've cried in multiple places), but never in my lifetime have I ever cried so much and been that moved. That night, as she talked about identity, Pastor Char showed the scene from *The Lion King* where Rafiki and Simba are by the water.

Simba looks into the water and says, "That's not my father; that's just my reflection."

Rafiki, the wise baboon he is, says, "No, look harder. You see, he lives in you."

Simba takes another look, this time seeing his father. Mufasa appears and speaks to his son. "Simba, you have forgotten me. You have forgotten who you are, and so forgotten me. Look inside yourself. You are more than what you have become. Remember, you are my son, the one true king! Remember who you are!"[9]

How many of us forget who we are? How many of us sometimes forget who our Father is? This short movie clip brought light to the fact that I was in a moment where I needed to remember who I am and remember who God is. I needed to take a moment to remember that all of this was getting figured out, and soon I would be in good health.

In just a few short minutes, I was shown that I need to remember that because God is a part of me, I am a part of him, and nothing is too hard for him. Therefore, if there is nothing too hard for him, there is nothing too hard for me because he is with me. As long as God is in my life, I will always come out of the flames in one piece.

That Sunday morning service was amazing as always. There were good words all around, and as we all received Communion, one song changed my life forever: "Show Me Your Face." I thought I was a mess after that movie clip from *The Lion King*, but hearing this song for the first time brought back feelings that I hadn't experienced in over a decade. I completely fell apart.

When my grandma passed away, "Here I Am Lord" was the song she chose to be sung at her funeral. For years after her passing, I would recognize the hymn number on the board at the front of the church, hear the introduction, and have to excuse myself. For years, I couldn't listen to that song because it hurt, and I didn't want to hurt. But because I didn't want to hurt, I never had a breakthrough, I never healed, and years later it caused me a great deal of pain and suffering.

We all received Communion that Sunday, one by one. One of my favorite parts about being a Christian is receiving the Holy Sacrament of the Eucharist. Even when I was Catholic, that was the one part of Mass that I thoroughly enjoyed because it was done in remembrance of the sacrifices that were made so that we could be saved and forgiven. It was to remember that our debts were paid on the cross, that he gave his body and shed his blood for us.

I didn't realize until coming to World Harvest Church that Communion wasn't a time to be sad and depressed. In fact, church in general wasn't a time to be sad and depressed. I always felt, growing up in the Catholic faith, that everything was a punishment. There wasn't happiness in the Catholic Church; at least, there wasn't in mine. You didn't see people talking before or after Mass. Everybody came and left quietly, and everybody always seemed so sad. You didn't dare smile, you didn't dare share a laugh, and anytime you'd make any sort of noise, you'd get a look from Mildred sitting in the pew across from you.

This is incredibly sad for me to admit, but my first time at World Harvest was actually a very uncomfortable experience. There are people singing, dancing, laughing, hugging, fainting, and speaking in tongues. That's a lot to digest when your entire faith was based on coming in, sitting down, and being quiet. I quickly learned that this wasn't a place to be quiet, and slowly but surely, I began to enjoy it. This was a place filled with love, joy, happiness, and an incredible amount of peace!

This was a place where people came to *worship* the King! This wasn't a place where people came to mourn; it was a place where people came to *celebrate*! A place where Jesus Christ is celebrated because he is no longer up on that cross! He rolled away the stone, and he isn't in the tomb anymore either! He died and rose again for you, and for me, and for every living soul on this earth so that we may experience his goodness and faithfulness! Someone had better be shouting AMEN right now!

I loved every moment. Never in a million years did I ever think that I would be there, praising the Lord because he is alive, and I'm forgiven! It was no longer a sad and angry "Look what he did for you. Look at what you made him do for you. You weren't worthy; you weren't deserving, but he died for you anyway!"

It was, and is now, a celebration: "HALLELUJAH! Look what he did for you! You weren't worthy—you weren't deserving—but he didn't care. He loved you so much that he did that for you. Praise Jesus! Amen."

Not long after receiving Communion that Sunday morning, a sharp pain presented from my stomach to my back. It was as if I had been stabbed and it came all the way through. I began to cry even more. I couldn't stop. Every ounce of my being was in so much pain. Emotionally, I was drained. Mentally, I was exhausted. Physically I wanted to lie down and curl up in a ball. The service ended, and I continued to cry.

I heard a voice in my right ear say, "Come forth. Your time has come," so I did exactly that. I approached Pastor Char at the altar, and she did something that I hadn't experienced in over a decade. She looked me dead in the eyes and began to sing, "Show me your face."

To her, it was probably normal, but for me, it was so much more.

My mom stopped singing to me after Grandma died. In fact, a lot of things stopped after Grandma died. I used to lie in bed every night as Mom brushed her fingers through my hair, singing, "You are my sunshine." She'd kiss my head, and there was always so much warmth and peace in that moment. After Grandma died, that warmth and peace left.

So, when Pastor Char started singing to me and kissed my head, I was brought back to that exact moment in my childhood. I felt as if I stopped breathing. I cried and screamed and eventually dropped to the floor.

I slowly returned to a seated position, completely in shock. My mouth felt like cotton. I felt as if I'd just left my body. And, believe it or not, I had some function in my left arm, which hadn't happened in weeks.

"That was the strongest one yet," I said, feeling the panicked look on my face.

I had been touched by the Holy Spirit multiple times in my few months of attending this church, but not like this. When I first attended church and heard about people getting touched by the Holy Spirit, I thought they were crazy, and sadly I was extremely judgmental.

When I first saw somebody hit the floor, I thought, "Well, anybody can flop to the floor and say it's the Holy Spirit." It's not until it happens to you, and there are six people waiting for you to wake up, placing their hands on you in prayer, that you realize, *Holy crap! What just happened?*

When I returned home, I jumped back into my comfy clothes, and as I changed my shirt, I noticed blood dripping from my abdomen. I didn't remember bumping into or getting hit with anything, but I also don't know how I got half the bruises on my body either. Anything was possible at this point. I wiped away the blood and found what appeared to be a small stab wound. *It doesn't hurt. It should hurt. What the heck is going on?* I put a bandage over it and made my way to the kitchen.

I sat down at the kitchen table and leaned forward to pick up my laptop off the floor.

"What happened to your back?" Mom grabbed my shirt to get a closer look.

"What do you mean, 'What's wrong with my back?"

I could feel a pit deep in my stomach. I had a good feeling as to exactly what she was talking about.

"There's blood on the back of your shirt. What happened?" She went back to the sink to finish the dishes.

"I must have bumped into something." I stood up quickly and began walking back down the hall.

No way. This is impossible. There is no possible way that this is happening. You've got to be kidding me! OK. Don't panic. It's going to be OK. Just look.

I looked at the back of my shirt, and she was right. I was bleeding. Scared to take off my shirt, I decided to just get it over with.

Ho—ly!

Just as there was a wound on my abdomen, there was a wound in the exact same spot on my back. *That's what I felt in church! I DID feel it. I felt it all!*

I created a group text to the ladies, Pastor Char included, who took care of me during that episode. "I've officially gone off the deep end."

I remember the first time Angie brought me to church. She knew I was uncomfortable, but she and everyone in the church were very sympathetic. I was never pushed to do anything I didn't feel comfortable doing. Besides, they knew one day I'd get there. I had already taken the first steps; now they just needed to walk me through the next ones before I bolted. My experiences this time made the chances of that happening slim.

After service, the prayer team stood at the front of the church, and anyone who wanted to receive prayer was able to come up and partake. I stared at those that went up but continued to stand still. *I really want to. I probably need to. No, not this time. I'm not ready.*

"Do you want to go up there?" Angie asked. She could see the questions in my eyes.

"No, thank you. I think just coming was enough for today," I kindly replied.

During the entire car ride home, I was kicking myself because I had actually wanted to receive prayer. Believe it or not, I missed it. I craved it.

The following Sunday, Angie and I attended again, and I didn't feel as uncomfortable. Halfway through worship, I closed my eyes and swayed back and forth to the beat of the music.

"Give me a sign, Lord. I'm really struggling here. Just please, give me a sign." The words left my mouth faster than my brain had time to process them.

A few minutes later, I felt a hand grab my right shoulder. I didn't want to open my eyes because if I opened them and there was nothing there, I was going to run out of the building screaming and probably never return. I took a deep breath and looked over to find Angie's hand firmly grasping my right shoulder.

"I don't know what it was, but I felt like a pressure cooker about ready to explode." She looked up with tears in her eyes.

With each passing moment, I realized what was happening: I was falling back in love with Jesus.

The following weekend, I had to work and had decided to go to the Saturday night service. It was only my third time, and the idea of going alone frightened me. I didn't know anybody, and I've never really been one to enjoy going to new places with new people by myself. I sat in the middle row, right-hand corner by myself and soaked it all in.

As I listened to the music, I still didn't really feel anything. I wanted to—I tried to—but it just didn't happen at that moment. Pastor Char grabbed the microphone, and as the worship team continued to sing, she invited those who needed prayer to come up to the front.

I sat there, watching person after person going up to receive prayer. *I want to; I really do. No, just stay seated. You don't need it.*

I sat there for a few seconds when a feeling came over me that I couldn't control. It was as if I lost complete control of my body, and someone had me on puppet strings.

What are you doing? SIT DOWN! I continued arguing with myself, but it was too late. Soon, I was at the front of the church with Pastor Char.

From the moment I first shook her hand and was introduced to her, I felt safe with her. The funny thing is that I've never been drawn to things that made me feel safe, especially people, because they never last. But for some reason, this time was different. Grabbing my right hand with one hand and my left shoulder with the other, she began to pray.

"I feel really weird. I don't like this. My heart is racing," I said, feeling faint.

"I know." She looked up for a brief second, smiled, and kept praying.

My mind was saying, *Listen, lady, I told you I felt uncomfortable. Why aren't you stopping?* But my heart said, *Relax. Relax. Let HIM work through her.*

She ended her prayer, gave me a hug, and I returned to my seat.

The worship music ended, and Pastor Char got up to the front and began to speak on "Overcoming the Orphan Mindset."[10] As I sat there that evening, it was as if everything that had ever been in my mind, heart, and brain for the past two decades was standing right in front of me, telling me everything that I needed to hear. I've never had an encounter like that.

"You can come sit over here. I won't bite." I heard her whisper from across the aisle.

I looked over, and there was a girl who looked very familiar, motioning for me to come sit by her. I got up and moved my things across the aisle, and it was as if we had been best friends since birth. Aren't those relationships incredible?

After service, I was talking with this beautiful woman when Pastor Char approached me with a few other women. I immediately felt as though I was going to be interrogated, and then I got the dreaded question: "Can we pray for you?"

I didn't want to be rude or come off judgmental, so I accepted. My heart sank, my palms began to sweat, and I could hear my heart beating in my ears. They all placed their hands on me, and in that moment, I felt what Angie had described. I felt like a pressure cooker ready to explode. I looked up at Pastor Char, and she had a concerned look on her face as her eyes grew big.

"Kinze. Honey, are you OK?" She had a concerned look on her face, but I didn't know what face to look at. There were too many of them.

Nope.

I felt the hands grab my shoulders as Pastor Char grabbed my feet and swung them up onto the chair. I could see them all and hear them all, but I couldn't move. I lay there on the chairs, my body shaking uncontrollably. I was terrified but could do absolutely nothing at that moment. I was glued to the chairs. About twenty minutes later, I returned to a seated position, wondering what had just happened.

Is this what everyone feels in those moments before they hit the spiritual deck? That was such a weird feeling, but it was kind of incredible. Yet, it was terrifying. I had passed out before, but this was different.

I got into my car and immediately called Angie. "Angie! You're never going to believe what happened! I felt it, Angie. I *definitely* felt it!"

"Kinze, slow down. What are you talking about?" she asked, sounding confused.

"Angie! That day you felt like a pressure cooker? It happened to me tonight. I passed out and everything!" I yelled into the phone.

I heard nothing but laughter coming from the other end of the line.

"Well, Kinze, I told you!" she said as she continued giggling on the other end.

"I know you told me, but I didn't believe you. I thought you were crazy!" I took a moment to catch my breath, and there was a space of silence before I could hear her little sniffle. I don't have to physically see Angie to know when she gets emotional. I just know by the sound of her voice.

She started to laugh again and said, "Guess we can be crazy together then, huh? I'm so glad you experienced that tonight. I'm sad that I missed it. Things are really looking up for you, Kinze. I'm so excited and proud of you! I love you!"

I ended the call and pulled over into an empty parking lot. I looked into the rearview mirror and just stared at myself in disbelief. *Did that really just happen? That really happened! No, it didn't. Yes it did. No it didn't. YES IT DID! There were witnesses.*

How was it that all of this was happening before my eyes in a matter of weeks? Was it possible that my overall health was improving? It *was* possible because it was happening. In fact, it was like I was becoming brand-spankin' new.

Chapter 11

DON'T WORRY; THIS IS JUST THE BEGINNING

Blessed are those who wash their robes, that they may have the right to the tree of life and may go through the gates into the city.

Revelation 22:14

"And yeah. That's my story, I guess." I sat there as the ladies from the cell group (a group that gathers together to worship the Lord on different nights of the week) stared at me.

"Kinze—Girl, you need to write a book!"

I felt my face turn red and laughed as if her suggestion was incredibly outrageous.

As I drove home that night, I remembered the vision I'd had about four years prior. The vision of *the* book. I remembered sitting on "Benchie," staring at the piece of paper before going into the office.

"Jen, I'm going to write a book," I said, sliding the piece of paper toward her.

On it was a sunset, and in big black lettering said, "McKinze Berg: Another One Welcomed Home."

"Well, when you write it, I want the first signed copy. Deal? So tell me. What's it about?" I stared at her as if she were speaking a foreign language.

Wait. You mean you're going to write a book, but you don't have a story?

I shrugged my shoulders. "No idea. I just have the title."

At first, she laughed at me, but then a serious look came over her face. "I'm sure you'll figure it out."

For four years, I completely forgot that writing a book was even a thought. So much had consumed my life that if I was going to write any sort of book, the title most certainly wouldn't have been *Another One Welcomed Home.*

I pulled into the driveway that night and stared at myself in the rearview mirror before getting out of the car to go inside. *You're going to write the book. You had the story all along. You just needed Jesus to finish it. You've found yourself, Kinze. You're doing the work, and you have a story to tell. And even after all of this, and when the book is finished, your story is not.*

I watched the tears form in my eyes as goosebumps formed on my arms. I went upstairs, pulled out my old college laptop from under the bed, blew the dust off, hit the Reset button, and turned it on. I created a brand-new account, opened the doc, and began to write.

The next morning, I woke up and sent a picture of the new cover to the group. "Well, guys, I guess I'm writing a book."

As I began writing, I realized that Jennifer was right this entire time. Jennifer, I can see you smiling and saying, "I told you so." You were right, OK? You were right that I had the story all this time, and I get it now. All those times I drew the pictures, wrote in the journals, or wrote notes in my phone, they weren't for nothing. In fact, it was quite the opposite. It was for everything. It was for this book so others could read this and say, "I want that!"

Writing this book has been a healing process for me. It forced me to realize that all those moments in my life that I thought I worked through, I didn't. This book forced me to relive my deepest darkest times and actually take time to feel those emotions as my fingers moved across the keyboard, writing every chapter. This book forced me to realize that this wasn't just a story; it was *my* story. And soon, people would finally know it.

If you recall, back in chapter 8, I shared about my traumatic brain injury experience and the long recovery process. What I failed to share in that chapter was what occurred that night I got home from the hospital—and what would occur for months following. That night, when I went to sleep, I ended up waking up at 3:14.

You're probably wondering, "Well, that's a little specific, isn't it?"

Don't worry. I thought the same thing. That day, I got up a little later in the morning and didn't really have an appetite, but I started getting hungry mid-afternoon. I stood in the kitchen, and when I looked at the times on the stove and microwave, they both read 3:14.

I didn't think anything of it until that night. I went to bed, and when I got up in the middle of the night to use the bathroom and looked at the alarm clock, there it was again in neon yellow numbers. 3:14. I came back to bed, absolutely irritated. *Why do I keep seeing 3:14?*

For years after the accident, I'd be up at 3:14 in the morning, and every afternoon when I'd look at the time, it was 3:14. You look at clocks and times all day long, but what are the chances that you'd see the exact time twice a day, every day, for years?

One night, I lay in bed, staring at the ceiling, thinking about 3:14. The accident happened on March 19, so that wasn't it. Mom and Dad's wedding anniversary is March 14, but that's not going to be something that keeps me up at night. *What is 3:14 . . . 3:14 . . . 3:14?. . . Was that the time of the accident? That has to be it! It sounds about right, but why would that continue to show up?*

I realized at that moment that it wasn't just about 3:14. For years, I'd had the same dream every single night, and to this day I remember it just as well as the original day itself. Every night, I was brought back to that moment of the accident. Every night, I'd get around that corner and watch myself fall, but just as I was about to hit my head, I'd wake up. *That's it. 3:14 is when I hit my head. It has to be.* I went on with life as usual, and over time, the dream went away, and I no longer would wake up in the middle of the night at 3:14, nor would I look at the time and see it in the afternoon.

From the moment after the accident, my health continued to decline. I often woke up absolutely exhausted, my moods were unpredictable, I'd be nauseated all the time, and I vomited several times a day. I was losing weight, couldn't keep food down, and was always needing to go to the hospital to get fluids or have tubes shoved down my nose for nutrition. I was dizzy all the time, and it got to the point where dying would have been better.

I met with all the surgeons and specialists and did all the tests, but anything that was drawn on the whiteboard wasn't going to work. The medications weren't working, the therapies weren't helping, and everybody was scratching their heads about what to do.

It was another long drive to Rochester early one morning, and the doctor came in and slowly sat down by her desk. "There's nothing we can do for you. I'm sorry. If we try to fix this, it's not going to be long-term. Unfortunately, the long-term solution would send you out in a body bag, and that's not a game we're willing to play. It would be over a fifty percent chance that you'd never make it off the table, and if you did, your quality of life would never be the same."

That day changed our lives forever. That day was March 14, 2023.

I never thought I'd be the same. I never thought *life* would be the same. Every day, I woke up hating being on this planet, praying every night that I'd be taken in my sleep. Every morning was the same: get up, throw on clothes, and watch the day go by. There was no life anymore. I was simply existing.

I clocked into work one morning and made my rounds to talk with Angie, who was still there from the night shift.

"Here, I want you to read this. Let me know what you think." She flipped through the pages before handing me the book.

Angie was the only person in my life at that point who never told me to "just pray on it more," or "just accept this and move on," or "look at the positives in your life."

Angie did something completely different. She sat in the mud with me instead of trying to fix everything or pull me out. She recognized that I had hit a rough patch in my life, that I was completely exhausted, and instead of trying to "fix it," she sat with me through it, saying in not so many words, "That's OK. We're not staying here. We're just going to take a little break." She continued to love me, and on her own time, she continued fulfilling her Christian duties by praying and asking God to help her help me.

Intercessory Prayer by Dutch Sheets. I looked at the cover and decided to give it a chance. I read the entire book in a matter of three days. It was wonderful! I not only recognized that Dutch Sheets is an amazing author, but I realized that Angie was the intercessor. I may not have realized it at that exact moment, but as time went on, I could see exactly what was happening. I wasn't returning to God on my own. He knew it was time for me to come home, so he went a different route. He used her to get to me. *Clever. Sneaky. But it worked.*

From the moment I pulled into the driveway leading to the cabin, my life was changed forever. My life may have changed before that, but I wasn't in a place to recognize it. However, I did recognize it at the cabin. I realized it the moment I stepped foot on that doormat.

I got up early that next morning after arriving to the cabin the night before, made my coffee, and went out to the patio to read. I didn't think I was out there that long, but it was long enough to watch the sun rise and feel the temperature spike. After going inside, I got out the frying pan, and started cracking a few eggs. 9:11. The time came across the digital clock in the kitchen. I sat down, ate, continued to worship, continued to read, spent hours outside, made supper, and settled down for the night. Before putting my phone on silent, I looked at the screen one last time before shutting it off—9:11.

That next morning was like deja vu: waking up early, watching the sun rise, feeling the temperature spike, making breakfast—9:11. *You've got to be kidding me, now what?* The day went on, I took my shower, got in bed, put my phone on silent mode, and saw the dreaded numbers as I turned the screen over for the night—9:11.

Just as I had gone stir crazy with 3:14, I started going stir-crazy with 9:11. *What happened on September 11, 2001 wasn't going to stick with me like this. I was three years old. I don't remember the event happening, I only ever heard about it. What happened on September 11 all the other years? Did something happen at 9:11 or on 9/11 at some point in my life?*

Sitting there, scratching my head, I was becoming more irritated as the days went on. Isn't it frustrating when you're trying to think of things or moments, and you can't remember what or when it happened? As the days went on, I continued to see 9:11, but over time, it didn't bother me. It was just another time of the day.

On Saturday August 26, 2023, I was up before everyone in the house. I grabbed a cup of coffee, sat on my bedroom floor, and began to read from my Bible daily verse app. I immediately giggled as I saw 3:14 from the book of Matthew. "But John tried to deter him, saying, 'I need to be baptized by you, and do you come to me?'"

I closed the app and opened my Bible to continue reading the chapter.

> Jesus replied, "Let it be so now; it is proper for us to do this to fulfill all righteousness." Then John consented.
>
> As soon as Jesus was baptized, he went up out of the water. At that moment heaven was opened, and he saw the Spirit of God descending like a dove and alighting on him. And a voice from heaven said, "This is my Son, whom I love; with him I am well pleased."

Later that afternoon, I sat down once again with my Bible and my journal. Breaking into the book of Exodus, I immediately stopped after about twenty minutes of reading. Feeling the color drain from my face, I began to get hot. My hands started to shake, and my eyes got wide.

Exodus 3:14: "I AM WHO I AM."

I closed the little purple Bible and sat there in a state of shock. *Holy crap.* Then, I opened the Bible and read it again. "I AM WHO I AM." Closing it again I finally put it aside.

I grabbed my phone and started messaging Angie. "3:14 wasn't just the time of the accident, and it's not just my parents' wedding anniversary. It's the day I had my appointment with the surgeon in Rochester, and she said that there was nothing we could do. Look at Exodus 3:14. 'I AM WHO I AM.' Angie, I was looking at it wrong the entire time!"

I sat there and stared at the phone in disbelief. *Wait a minute. 9:11. It's not a time, it's a date. 9:11, September 11th. It's not something that happened. It's something that's going to happen!*

I opened up my conversation with Pastor Char, and began to type: "What are you doing September 11?"

About an hour later, she replied back. "Hey there. I actually will be traveling home from Peru that day."

Dang it. "Is Bob going with you? This is going to be crazy, and I can't wait to tell you the story, but do you think he would baptize me that day? Or if he can't, is there someone that could?" I kept the conversation open, nervously waiting for a response.

"I can certainly ask. I'm not sure if he would be available, but it's possible that someone else would be available. We do have baptisms scheduled for the first Sunday in October, I think. But if that date is significant for you, then maybe you can arrange something?" she replied back.

She was right, it had to be September 11, so I opened my conversation with Amy and began to type. "Morning darling! Question for you . . . Would you be available Monday, September 11, any time, to do a baptism?"

The phone was barely out of my hands before she already had a reply. "Good morning! I am always up for a baptism!"

Jumping out of my chair with excitement, I typed aggressively on the screen "This is going to sound crazy, but how about I go under at 9:11 on 9/11?"

"That could work! I'm so excited for you!" she replied, following the statement with a laughing emoji and prayer hands.

I set the phone down and paced the hallway. *This is it. THIS . . . IS . . . IT!*

The following weekend, I returned to church. An overwhelming amount of peace overtook my body as I entered the church. My heart felt full of joy. As I sat there waiting for worship to begin, the familiar feeling of warmth came over me. *Good morning to you too. Thank you for being here with me this morning.*

I had my usual morning conversations with some of the churchgoers and prepared for worship.

As I sat down, everything went into slow motion. I closed my eyes, continuing to listen to the music, seeing nothing but the back of my eyelids. With my eyes still closed, I could see something coming closer. It got closer and closer, and in red letters "Ezekiel 9:11" appeared. Not yet getting to the book of Ezekiel in my studies, I pulled out my red Bible and turned right to it. "Then the man in linen with the writing kit at his side brought back word, saying, 'I have done as you commanded.'" I must have reread that verse at least ten times before jumping up to hand it to Angie to read.

"Yes, you have," she said, wiping the tears from her eyes.

After service had ended, I packed up my things and stood there watching each person go up to receive prayer.

"Come on, Kinze!" I looked up to see one of my favorite ladies standing at the front of the church, motioning for me to come to her. "Yep! I'm talking to you. Get up here!"

I went up to her, and she gently laid her hands on my shoulders.

"How's the arm? Let's see." She grabbed my arm, trying to test its range of motion.

Just a few weeks prior, my left arm had been completely dead as if it weren't even attached to my body. That weekend, and the weekend prior, after much prayer, I was able to open and close my hand and lift my forearm. Although it was very weak. And I couldn't grasp anything or lift my forearm without a significant amount of pain. It was progress! *Thank you, Jesus*!

"YES! Yes, yes, yes!" She started jumping up and down with excitement.

She closed her eyes, placed her hands back on my shoulders, and began to pray. After she was finished, she wiped the tears from her eyes, gave me a big hug, took a step back to take a deep breath, and said words that gave me chills down my spine. "Don't worry. This is just the beginning."

Chapter 12
THIS IS GOODBYE

Then the man in linen with the writing kit at his side brought back word, saying, "I have done as you commanded."

Ezekiel 9:11

When I was eighteen, I got a butterfly tattoo on my left foot. At the time, there was no meaning. There was no rhyme or reason behind it; I simply received satisfaction from sitting in a chair, getting stabbed repeatedly with needles. When the tattoo artist finished, he seemed really proud of his work, but I personally wasn't overly thrilled. They aren't original; everyone has—or knows somebody with—a butterfly tattoo. For years, I wanted it gone, but I knew that getting it removed was going to hurt worse than when I got it, so I left it.

One Sunday morning, Pastor Char stood in front of the church and preached a sermon titled "Season of Transition." The biggest lesson I received that day was that it was time for me to crawl into the cocoon and die. I know it sounds crazy and probably doesn't make any sense, but just hang on. I'm getting there.

I'd been a caterpillar long enough. Now, it was time to go through the motions and break free to enter my life as a butterfly. Perhaps you're reading this wondering, *Does she always go off on random tangents? Has her brain been checked?* Yes, it has. And don't worry; we're taking care of it.

That Sunday, she preached that "the Word of God is designed to make you into a butterfly, not to keep you as a caterpillar." She said if we take the Word of God, read it, and hope to be a butterfly but continue to live as a caterpillar, it will do absolutely nothing for us. "You must take the Word of God, believe the Word of God, wrap yourself in a cocoon with the Word of God, and then what happens? What happens to the caterpillar when it goes into that cocoon? It dies! We die, so that we can allow who we truly are to come out. When we believe like Jesus, we will act like Jesus!"[11]

If this still doesn't make sense to you, you're not alone. Please remain patient, it will make sense here shortly.

When I lay down for bed that night, I couldn't stop thinking about that sermon. I intentionally pulled out my cell phone to rewatch the message on YouTube, but you're never going to believe this: I got sidetracked. As I scrolled through the world of Pinterest, I came across one of my favorite pages: Tattoo Ideas. I was always looking for my next tattoo. I enjoyed it. It brought me a significant amount of joy and pain all at the same time.

As I was scrolling, I saw a picture of a butterfly tattoo located on someone's back, and underneath it read *Tutto ha il suo tempo.* Good thing that I'm typing this because if I were to speak it, I would completely butcher the phrase. I'm not Italian, don't speak a lick. It's not even in my Ancestry.com results. But in English, it translates to "Everything has its time."

I knew then that my decision to keep my butterfly tattoo wasn't for nothing. After all these years, it was finally going to have meaning.

When I got the tattoo, I was a caterpillar that had no idea that it had the DNA of a butterfly. I didn't know that a transformation was going to happen and that the caterpillar inside of me was going to disintegrate. I had no idea that I had already crawled into the cocoon and didn't realize I was in the process of dying. Well, I knew I was in the process of dying, but I didn't think it'd be like this.

Have you ever taken time to look at a caterpillar? You might say, "No. It's a caterpillar." Exactly! Rarely does anyone ever look at a caterpillar and say, "Oh my goodness, would you look at that caterpillar? How beautiful!"

If you do, that's amazing. I'm proud of you for noticing the small things in life. But eventually, that caterpillar dies, and this transformation begins. If you've never seen this process in third-grade science class, it's beautiful! The same goes in life. To see somebody—or to experience it yourself—completely disintegrate, hit rock bottom, wrap themselves in this cocoon, shutting out the world to find who God made them to be, and finally have that breakthrough! How beautiful it is to be reborn and get to be there for it!

I've witnessed a lot of beautiful things in my career, but one of the most beautiful things you can witness is the birth of a child. It's extremely painful for the person going through it, but the process and result are incredible! Through our physical birth, we enter this temporary world, and to gain access to a more eternal reality—the kingdom of God—we need that experience of spiritual birth. And why can't it be equally as beautiful? We all experience this at different points in our lives—some later than others—but we need to experience this transformation to prepare ourselves for the next world.

The process can, and probably will, hurt a lot. It can, and it will, be equally beautiful, but it can only happen on God's time. Isaiah 43:2 says, "When you pass through the waters, I will be with you." It doesn't say *if* you pass through. It doesn't say *if* you walk through. It says *when* you. This was not only God's promise to Israel, but also his promise to you.

You will go through troubles and trials in your life, and it's going to be hard sometimes, but if you let him, he will be *with* you through it *all.* All does not mean just from the hours of 9:00 a.m. to 5:00 p.m. on Monday through Friday. All means one hundred percent of the time. All means every single second, of every single minute, of every single hour, of every single day.

God will not put you in a situation that is out of his will for your life, nor will he lead you anywhere that he isn't or won't be. If you're at a point in your life where you're thinking, *This is too hard,* or *I'm done,* or, *I can't do this,* that is not God. When we turn to Jesus Christ, we can do things we never dreamed were possible. We survive things we wish we didn't have to face. When we turn to Jesus Christ, he is there with us. There is nothing that is too hard for him, and because nothing is too hard for him, there is nothing too hard for us. Whether you feel him and see his works or not, he's got you. Let go and trust him.

I woke up on the morning of September 11, 2023, did my Bible and devotional readings, and made my way to the kitchen to pour a cup of coffee. As I walked down the hallway into the living room, I saw a familiar face standing in the window, staring across the street. Grabbing my mug, I went up behind her, placed my hand on her shoulder, and kissed the top of her head.

"You're going to be alright, kiddo." I sat down on the couch in silence and observed her next actions.

"What did I do?" she screamed.

You didn't do anything.

"I can do better!" she screamed.

You're a child. You're doing what you can.

"I can be better!" she screamed.

You're a child. You don't need to be anything but that.

I watched the tears roll down her face as she stared at the house across the street. I got up and stood behind her, both of our reflections merging in the window. "You did nothing wrong. You don't know this now, but it wasn't supposed to be this way. It should have never happened this way, but it did, and although it's going to be one heck of a ride, you're going to be OK. It's not, and never was your fault."

I put my cup in the sink, grabbed my keys, and walked down the stairs to put on my shoes.

As I backed out of the driveway, I saw my nine-year-old self standing in the window, tears continuing to fall down my cheek. I could hear my younger screams from the top of the driveway, and it hurt just as bad as it did decades prior. I pulled back into the driveway and went inside again. I didn't want to take her with me, but something in my heart told me that I needed to. Something in my heart told me that I couldn't leave her behind, so we got in the car and drove up the road.

I entered the church that morning and sat in the chair located in the back middle row. I closed my eyes and felt the seat beneath me, my bare feet touching the ground. As the rest of the world remembered a tragedy that occurred twenty-two years prior, I was preparing for a celebration: a new life. As I sat in prayer, I was led to Ephesians 2:1–5.

> As for you, you were dead in your transgressions and sins, in which you used to live when you followed the ways of this world and of the ruler of the kingdom of the air, the spirit who is now

> at work in those who are disobedient. All of us also lived among them at one time, gratifying the cravings of our flesh and following its desires and thoughts. Like the rest, we were by nature deserving of wrath. But because of his great love for us, God, who is rich in mercy, made us alive with Christ even when we were dead in transgressions—it is by grace you have been saved.

Today was the day. The day that my life would change forever. The day the little girl that lived inside of me for so many years was going to be set free in the middle of the cold, shallow waters. There was a little over an hour to wait, so I went out to the lobby to find a pen and paper, walked to the front of the church, knelt, and began to write:

> Dear younger self,
>
> You didn't know. You were just a child. You tried to grow up faster than you had to, and it wasn't your job. You don't know this yet, but it was never supposed to be that way. It just unfortunately happened that way. But the good news is that you're going to reach a time in your life when you'll realize that it wasn't for nothing. You'll get to a point where you realize that there's a real world out there, that you don't have to hide anymore, and you're going to become a much better person because of everything that happened. I love you, and I am so proud of you and who you've

become. You've finally found your way, kid, and it's only going to go up from here. I forgive you. He forgives you. Now it's time to forgive yourself.

Love you, kiddo,

K

I folded the piece of paper and placed it in my pocket. For so long, I had my goodbye prepared, but never in a million years did I think my goodbye would look like this. When I pictured saying goodbye, I imagined it was going to be from a hospital bed surrounded by friends and family. I never thought that I was going to be saying goodbye in a river, healed and forgiven. I imagined that somebody would be sharing my story as a part of their eulogy. I never thought that I'd be sitting at my kitchen table, telling you the story myself.

I pulled into the parking lot by the bridge and waited for the rest of the ladies to arrive. It was a beautiful, yet chilly, September day. The water was still. The light breeze rustled the leaves, and this overwhelming amount of peace surrounded the area. One by one, they all pulled in behind me and jumped out of their cars.

"These are going to be the longest four minutes of our lives," Amy said as we patiently waited for the minutes to pass by.

While we waited, I shared a short testimony. The ladies shared kind words and words of wisdom, and then it was finally time—9:11.

I waded out into the cold water with Angie and Amy and prepared my goodbyes. In a matter of seconds, my entire life flashed before my eyes. I got into the water and sat down, chills running up and down my spine, my breath becoming shallow. The water may have been cold, and my body may have entered a small state of shock, but oddly enough, I wasn't cold. In fact, I felt the complete opposite. My extremities may have been turning blue, but my heart was on fire, and I could feel the warmth and presence of the Holy Spirit pumping through my veins.

With Angie on my left and Amy on my right, I closed my eyes and breathed in every word spoken: "In your name, as she goes down, she's not only going to die to her flesh but is going to rise from the dead of Christ in a new nature, a new body, and a new soul. She will not only be baptized with water but the Holy Spirit, and it is going to infiltrate her heart, her mind, and her body. Baptism not just with water but with the Holy Spirit and with fire. In the name of Jesus, we baptize you in the name of the Father, the Son, and the Holy Ghost!"

The time was 9:11 on September 11, 2023. The time that I was submerged in water, died, and had my sins wiped clean. The time that I was resurrected to the new life I have in Christ. As I hit the water that day, I said goodbye to the little girl that had been trapped inside for so long. As I hit the water, I let go of her hand and watched her float away. I returned to the top, but she did not. This was goodbye.

I watched her tear-filled eyes lock with mine. *This is goodbye. This is goodbye to all those who never believed in you. This is goodbye to the doctors who said you'd never live to see thirty or eat normally ever again. This is goodbye to those who shattered your heart over and over again and made you feel unworthy. This is goodbye to those who made you feel that you could never be loved or see the good in yourself, never be able to love yourself. This is goodbye to those who said you couldn't be saved. You are saved. You've been saved all this time. By his stripes you are saved, and you are healed!*

I got up out of the water and took the breath of a lifetime. I couldn't describe the feeling. I'd never experienced a feeling like that before. I felt incredibly light. Let me ask you this: Have you ever been weighed down in life? I'm not talking about being weighed down with a heavy heart or feeling weighed down by the world. I'm talking about physically being weighed down. Have you ever sat on the couch in the middle of winter and couldn't seem to get warm—you were cold to the bone—so you decided to pile every blanket you could find on top of every ounce of your body?

It feels heavy, doesn't it? How does it feel when you remove each one of those blankets? With each blanket you remove, the weight gets lighter and lighter, right? That's exactly how this felt. I felt as if I had just removed twenty-five years of blankets from my entire body, and I felt free.

I got into my car and began to drive home, but I had to make a pitstop. I pulled over into an empty parking lot and took out the white envelope that I had found tucked away in an old notebook I used for therapy—back when I first started. A letter written in 2019 to my future self—yes, four years *to the day* from when I was baptized.

To: My future self

From: McK19

Monday, September 11, 2019

Dear future self,

Today was a good day, and I'm sure that whatever you did was amazing! I'm proud of you, so take this time to be proud of yourself! Can you see it now? It wasn't for nothing. I told you so! Everything that has happened in your life, every trouble, every trial, every obstacle: it wasn't for nothing. I'm proud of you, and who've you become. You've done and are doing more things right now in your life than most people do in an entire lifetime, and it's only going to get better. You didn't know this when you wrote this, and you still probably haven't realized it yet (maybe you have), but you're a very stubborn and impatient person (don't worry; you're figuring it out; it's OK). You like things to be done on your time, and that's not how this works.

When you read this letter, you'll have realized that, amongst other things. You'll still be your stubborn self from time to time (more often than not), but I don't think that is going to change anytime soon. You like to keep things interesting and keep the Lord on his toes (along with everyone else), but that's OK because there's always a few loose chickens in his coop. Just remember that even though you get loose every now and then, you're still his, so always remember to come back home. Keep doing amazing things! I love you, and I'm proud of you!

Much love and many blessings,

Another One Welcomed Home

ACKNOWLEDGMENTS

Never in a million years did I think I would be writing a book, let alone a testimonial. Growing up, and even in recent years, I can't count the number of times I heard, "Girl, the number of lives you have touched and are going to touch with your story is going to be overwhelming. I hope you're ready!"

Newsflash. I wasn't ready, but I made myself ready. The birth of this story was a very painful one, but it was also the most rewarding, and I am so honored that I was able to share this experience with all of you.

I couldn't have done this by myself. I'm so thankful for my circle of friends, family, and friends who became family along the way to support me on this beautiful and incredible journey.

To my heavenly Father. Thank you for leaving the ninety-nine to come and find me. Again. For sending people into my life to save me, even though I didn't realize what you were doing because I was so far from you at that exact moment. Thank you for never giving up on me and for welcoming me back with open arms. Thank you for your endless love and overwhelming amount of patience. Thank you for everything that you are, Father God, and for everything that you have done so that I may have this intimacy and relationship with you. You are the Alpha and Omega, the beginning and the end, the way maker, the miracle worker, the promise keeper, and a lamp unto my feet that directs all my paths. I love you, Lord.

To my parents. Thank you for always believing in me. Even when the goal, or thought, seemed so outrageous. You knew that if I wanted it, I was going to go for it, with or without your approval. I'm sorry that you have yet to find the manual that shows you how to handle me, but I don't think that is a manual you are ever going to find. I love you to the moon and beyond. Thank you for everything.

To my sister, Morgan. You are the light of my life. Our lives have had so many changes, but the one thing that has remained constant is our love and support for one another. I'm beyond grateful and blessed that God paired us together as siblings and as best friends. I love you.

To my therapist, "Jennifer Zubell." (You know who you are.) When I met you in 2018, I swore up and down that I wasn't going to be someone who saw a therapist. I swore up and down that I wasn't going to become one of those people who felt their feelings. Well. Thanks for ruining that for me. I'M KIDDING! I'm so thankful for you and our time together. I'm thankful to be one of those "shrink-seeing people," and I'm even more thankful to be one of those "emotional, feely" people. You did that for me. You've done SO much for me, and you will always hold a special place in my heart. I love you.

To my "Mama in Christ," Angie Shipman. There aren't enough pages in this book for what I have to say to you, but I will continue to remind you every single day of our lives how grateful I am for you. You sat *with* me in the darkest season of my life, but you also pulled me *out* of the darkest season of my life and said, "We've been here long enough. It's time to get up." God placed you in my life and made you the intercessor. I relented, and it was all up from that moment on. Thank you. I love you forever!

To Pastor Char, Pastor Bob, and the entire World Harvest Church. Thank you for seeing me in ways that nobody, including myself, has ever seen me. For making me feel and think in ways that I never dreamed were possible. Thank you for bringing me up in the church, leading me, guiding me, helping me soar, and showing me what it means to be a child of God. Thank you for leading by example, for opening my eyes and heart to new experiences that have never been seen before. Thank you for providing a healing touch to every inch of this body. A touch that, through the grace of God, released the inner demons that were housed in this body for over two decades. I am free! Thank you. I love you!

To my circle of friends who have become family. Thank you for staying by my side through every season, no matter how dark that season got. If you turn to the Gospel of Mark, you will read about how Jesus healed a man suffering from paralysis. Jesus healed the man of his condition because of his friends' faith. It was because of your faith, your prayers, your love, your support, and your healing touch that I was able to find my way back to Jesus so that I may be completely healed. From the bottom of my heart, thank you. I love you.

NOTES

1 Charlie Mason, "Fifteen Years After Daytime's Most Out-There Drama Aired Its Last Episode, We Look Back at a Soap That Never Failed to Stir Our Passions—for Better *and* Worse!," *Soaps* blog, August 7, 2023, https://soaps.sheknows.com/soaps/news/604802/passions-cancelled-soap-last-episode-anniversary-photos/.

2 Sian Beilock PhD, "Flocking to the Familiar under Stress," *Psychology Today*, June 15, 2011, https://www.psychologytoday.com/us/blog/choke/201106/flocking-the-familiar-under-stress/.

3 "What is Gastroschisis?," Cincinnati Children's Hospital Health Library, accessed March 4, 2024, https://www.cincinnatichildrens.org/health/g/gastroschisis.

4 John Kanell, "Devil's Food Cake," Preppy Kitchen (website), March 31, 2022. https://preppykitchen.com/devils-food-cake/.

5 *Matilda*, directed by Danny Devito (Culver City, CA: TriStar Pictures, 1996), DVD.

6 Roya Shabkhizan, et al, "The Beneficial and Adverse Effects of Autophagic Response to Caloric Restriction and Fasting," Advances in nutrition (Bethesda, Md.) vol. 14,5 (2023): 1211-1225, doi:10.1016/j.advnut.2023.07.006, accessed April 3, 2024 (National Library of Medicine), https://www.ncbi.nlm.nih.gov/pmc/articles/PMC10509423/.

7 Brady Holmer, "Water Fasting: All You Need To Know," *HVMN*, November 14, 2019, https://hvmn.com/blogs/blog/biohacking-water-fasting-all-you-need-to-know.

8 "Pancreatitis," Johns Hopkins Medicine (website), accessed April 3, 2024, https://www.hopkinsmedicine.org/health/conditions-and-diseases/pancreatitis.

9 Pastor Char Pittman, "Remember Who You Are," sermon, YouTube, uploaded by World Harvest Church, August 21, 2023, https://www.youtube.com/watch?v=xxv2KTej-pY&t=1082s.

10 Pastor Char Pittman, "Overcoming The Orphan Mindset," YouTube, uploaded by World Harvest Church, June 5, 2023, https://www.youtube.com/watch?v=K8LAcsguVsM.

11 Pastor Char Pittman, "Season of Transition," YouTube, uploaded by World Harvest Church, May 22,2023. https://www.youtube.com/watch?v=Ewb6TWlz8Pw&t=2612s.

Kinze Berg is a registered respiratory therapist by trade, but her biggest and most important title is child of God. She is a daughter, writer, musician, evangelist and minister in training, and trauma survivor. Born and raised in the small town of New Auburn, Wisconsin, she has well over a decade's worth of experience dedicating her life to serving her community and heavenly Father. Originally raised in the Catholic faith, Kinze ventured off and found God in a new and improved way and was spiritually born again into the World Harvest Church in Rice Lake, Wisconsin, on May 21, 2023. She gave her life to Christ through water baptism on September 11, 2023, and continues her journey day by day to accomplish all that God has called her to do.

www.ingramcontent.com/pod-product-compliance
Lightning Source LLC
LaVergne TN
LVHW090523110826
845146LV00003B/959